Days
of
POWER

{ Part One }

For further information:

The Kabbalah Centre
155 E. 48th St., New York, NY 10017
1062 S. Robertson Blvd., Los Angeles, CA 90035

1.800.Kabbalah
www.kabbalah.com

First Edition, September 2005
Printed in USA
ISBN 1-57189-354-7

Design: Hyun Min Lee

Days of POWER

{ Part One }

www.kabbalah.com™

R A V   P. S.   B E R G

Days of Power is advanced Kabbalah. These are the words and teachings of a genuine Kabbalist, and while their meaning is not always obvious upon the first reading, the act of struggling to penetrate their truths will reveal tremendous Light in your life.

Acknowledgments

For my wife, Karen. In the vastness of cosmic space and the infinity of lifetimes, it is my bliss to be your soul mate and to share a lifetime with you.

$\mathcal{Table\ of}$ CONTENTS

Foreword

s I write this introduction to *Days of Power*, Rosh Hashanah is just a few weeks away. For me, this is an amazing moment. I know that, for the first time in history, the meaning of Rosh Hashanah and the other holidays will be fundamentally transformed. And as people's understanding of the holidays transforms, lives will also be transformed.

It is truly a gift to this generation that the Rav has revealed these secrets. Of course, the Rav has been revealing the wisdom of creating miracles for four decades. Sometimes, like with *Days of Power*, what we receive seems to be manifested in physical objects that we can touch or hold in our hands. Other times what we receive are the unseen connections with the Light, beyond the reach of our senses but with the power to eliminate chaos from our lives. The task of a Kabbalist is to reveal, and sometimes the task is to keep hidden.

One fact can't be concealed: All the wisdom that we teach at the Kabbalah Centre comes from the Rav, and his teachings are inseparable from his life.

Every day that we are in the Rav's presence is a day of power. With a book like the one you now hold in your hands, we can be in his presence always.

Yehuda Berg

Introduction

$\mathcal{T}$he title of this book, *Days of Power*, was chosen very carefully. Over the years, many books have been written about holidays and their spiritual meanings—and virtually all of them, I believe, could have been titled "Days of Memory," or perhaps "Days of Commemoration." The kabbalistic perspective expressed in *Days of Power*, however, is something entirely different from what we're used to. It goes far beyond either secular or conventionally religious interpretations of what holidays really are.

This is a very important point. In the everyday world, our concept of holidays is based on remembering, memorializing, and paying homage to some event in the past. Patriotic holidays such as the Fourth of July or Memorial Day, for example, commemorate the signing of the Declaration of Independence in 1776, and honor the men and women who died in the nation's wars. A traditional understanding of religious holidays follows the same principle: Christmas is the birthday of Jesus Christ; Passover is a remembrance of the Israelites' escape from Egyptian bondage; and Purim is the anniversary of their salvation from a genocidal plot. And certain holidays, of course, are simply a recognition of turning-point moments in the calendar, such as the New Year celebration of *Rosh Hashanah*.

Kabbalah, however, absolutely and completely rejects remembrance or recognition as the basis of holidays. In place of commemoration, a kabbalist focuses on *connection*—that is, the opportunity to tap into the unique energies that exist at the specific points in time that we call holidays. With this is mind, the meaning of the title *Days of Power* becomes clear. The holidays are literally power sources that we can access using the teachings and tools of Kabbalah. Those tools include prayers, ceremonies, *The Bible*, *The Zohar*, and continuing study and understanding of what God really intends for us—which is, by the way, nothing less than complete happiness and total freedom from any form of unhappiness, including death itself.

The concept of holidays as Days of Power—as points of potential connection with specific forms of energy—is the key premise of this book. In addition to this, several other fundamental concepts need to be clarified here at the start.

Most readers will notice, for example, that the holidays discussed in *Days of Power* are the holidays normally considered

"Jewish holidays." Yet that phrase appears nowhere in these pages. In fact, I have made a focused effort to make it clear that these holidays, like all the tools and teachings of Kabbalah, belong to all of humankind. Just as no one would say that the energy of gravity is a Jewish force, the energies of the various holidays are neither Jewish, Christian, Buddhist, or Hindu. They are simply basic aspects of the way the universe works, and they are beyond identification with any nation or religion.

In order to make the distinction between conventional Judaism and Kabbalah as clear and consistent as possible, I've also used terms such as "Israelite" and "people of Israel" throughout these pages. Occasionally, the term "chosen people" does occur in connection with the Israelites, but it's very important to understand exactly what this means. It does not mean a nationality. Kabbalah teaches that the people of Israel are those human beings who, at Mount Sinai, received the infinitely powerful package of energy called the *Torah*. They chose to accept the spiritual system. And, as always in Kabbalah, this was not a moment in ancient history but rather an event that each of us can and should reprise in our own lives. In this sense, everyone who accepts the tools and teachings of Kabbalah that God intends for us is an Israelite. But that's not all: Every Israelite also accepts the responsibility of sharing those tools and teachings. This is the real meaning of "chosen people:" It is not that the people have *been* chosen; it is that the people *have* chosen.

You, no matter who you are, can make that choice right now. This is totally unrelated to the religion in which you were raised, or the country where you were born, or any other fact about you. To explain this, I often use the metaphor of turning on a light switch to banish darkness from a dark room. Anyone can turn on the light. The electricity doesn't know or care about the details of your identity. What's more, you don't need to understand physics or electrical engineering in order to flip the switch or to benefit from that action. Increased knowledge can enhance your appreciation of what takes place, but that's yet to come. The all-important first step is simply understanding that the opportunities described in this book are not just available to you, but divinely intended for you. The rest is between you and that metaphorical light switch.

One final point. As I've said, Kabbalah is not religion, and to make that clear I've avoided using words that have clear religious associations. But the ultimate religious word, God, does appear many times in *Days of Power*. Although God is spoken of in human terms throughout the biblical narrative or in the commentaries on *The Bible*, Kabbalah definitely does not understand God as a man on a cloud, a woman riding in a chariot, or any other anthropomorphic form. This is made very clear in *The Bible*'s original Hebrew, where the word "God" is designated by a number of different words, including *"Adonai," "Elohim,"* and *Hashem."* Each of these words expresses a different aspect of God—a different energy. Sometimes this energy is one of mercy and forgiveness; at other points in *The Bible*, there is anger and severity.

But here is the key kabbalistic point: it is *we ourselves* who determine how the energy flows down. To understand this, consider the fact that electricity is always present in the wiring of a house. If a person recklessly chooses to put his finger in a wall socket, he will get a shock—the cause of which was his own action. On the other hand, if the same person plugs a toaster in the wall socket, he will get a piece of toast. In both cases, it would be foolish to "blame" or "credit" the nature of electricity for the consequence of the actions. Like electricity, gravity, or even nuclear energy, the power of the Creator is infinite, unlimited potential. How will that potential manifest itself? We ourselves make that decision in every moment of our lives.

Always and forever, God gives us the effect we need based on the cause we have set in motion. If we need God's presence in a certain form of energy, it is the nature of God to fulfill that need. But the ultimate purpose always remains the same: to move us toward total freedom from chaos, pain, illness, and death.

That is the purpose of the holidays, and it is also the intention of this book. May *Days of Power* help bring you the joy and fulfillment that are your true destiny.

The Truth Behind
VIRGO (*ELUL*)

very powerful kabbalistic prayer consists of only a few words: "Lead me in the correct path." Throughout our lives, the spiritual meaning of the months and the holidays can be a powerful tool for finding and following that path. Traditionally, the month of *Elul* is a time for repentance (*Teshuvah* in Aramaic), for *Elul* is followed immediately by *Rosh Hashanah* and the Days of Awe in the month of *Tishrei*. *Elul* is dedicated to introspection and self-scrutiny, which together involve taking a closer look at what has happened over the preceding ten months. At this time each year, Israelites the world over gather to ensure their destinies on the Day of Judgment.

The Book of Formation, composed by Abraham the Patriarch, is the first kabbalistic document. There it is written, "He appointed the letter *Resh*, and bestowed upon it a crown, and to it He assigned Mercury. He appointed the letter *Yud*, and bestowed upon it a crown, and to it He assigned Virgo in the world and *Elul* in the year." The phrase "bestowed upon it a crown" indicates that these Aramaic letters are the seed of the planets or signs they created. They are also the seeds of the channels that connect the planets to the *Sfirah* of *Keter*.

But Kabbalah teaches that the month of *Elul*, and the *Teshuvah* (repentance) that we undertake during that month and that culminates at *Rosh Hashanah*, has even greater purpose and meaning. According to *The Zohar*, *Teshuvah* is not just a practice whereby the Israelites ask forgiveness from the Creator. The biblical People of Israel are the "chosen people" only in the sense that they are the channels for bringing the tools and teachings of Kabbalah into the world. For centuries, there has been a misconception that at the Revelation on Mount Sinai, the Torah was given to the Israelites alone. *The Zohar* explains that this is, in fact, a mistaken notion; Israelites are, in fact, defined as people who are conscious vessels for the Light. The holiday of *Rosh Hashanah* is intended for all the peoples of the world. Indeed, all of the Torah's hidden wisdom and all kabbalistic festivals exist for humanity as a whole.

Repentance, in a kabbalistic sense, has nothing to do with asking forgiveness. A conventional understanding of repentance would suggests that wrongful behavior is acceptable throughout the rest of the year, because on *Rosh Hashanah* we can simply go into the nearest synagogue and ask for forgiveness. In this way, it is thought, we can evade the consequences of whatever we might have done over the past 12 months. But can we really expect to be pardoned for our sins merely by murmuring prayers on a certain holiday?

This is not the way to right the wrongs of the past year. What, then, is the "correct path" in which Kabbalah can lead us? What is the true meaning of *Teshuvah*?

The Zohar's cryptic answer is this: "When the *Hei* goes back to the *Vav*." Accurate interpretation of this passage informs us that all the damage we may cause over the course of a year takes place only because we have disconnected from the Creator's Light. In Aramaic, תשובה (*Teshuvah*) is actually *Tashuv Hei*. The ה (*Hei*), as the last of the four letters that make up the Tetragrammaton, alludes to the realm of *Malchut*—which should connect with the Tetragrammaton's first three letters, altogether representing the Tree of Life. Through this union of letters we may merit the revelation of Light that will facilitate the correction of the damage we have caused.

We can now see that *Teshuvah* is not just a religious ritual or a traditional recitation of prayers. Rather, it is a fundamental and far-reaching journey to the source of spiritual energy for the entire world. Recognizing this connection is in itself a revelation of great Light—and in the presence of the Light, darkness vanishes.

We do not need force or violence to destroy chaos, nor can we destroy it by those means. Even the defeat of the Nazi regime in the Second World War did not succeed in driving chaos from the world. Wars, disease, accidents, and hardship remain in the daily experience of all humanity to this very day. Over the generations, there have been many wars and revolutions with the purpose of freeing the masses and offering them the potential to live happily. Yet the problems that are ascribed to dictatorships stubbornly persist even after the dictators' fall.

Here the teachings of *The Zohar* are striking in their simplicity: Do not fight the darkness, for your battle against darkness has no chance of success. Instead, turn on the Light and the darkness will disappear. Dedicate your efforts to the revelation and dissemination of Light through the spiritual work of *Teshuvah*. Bringing the Creator's Light into our lives is the only way to remove all aspects of chaos.

The most powerful channel for Light is the Tetragrammaton, and *Teshuvah* is the means for connecting to this channel. The letter ו (*Vav*) represents the part of the spiritual world that is called *Zeir Anpin*. The final *Hei* in the Tetragrammaton represents the physical reality with which our minds and our five senses are familiar. The rejuvenating connection between the letter *Hei* and the letter *Vav* bring about a great revelation of Light on the physical plane. *The Zohar* urges us to meditate on this connection.

We can also renew our connection to the Light by converting our material consciousness—that is, by transforming the desire to receive for ourselves alone into the spiritual consciousness of *Zeir Anpin*, which is receiving for the sake of sharing. This change in consciousness is equal to a journey faster than the speed of Light—a journey "back to the future." In order to understand this, however, we must first examine a few aspects of the month of *Elul* and the sign of Virgo.

The internal quality of the sign of Virgo is virginity, meaning originality and integrity. A virginal thing is something that has not gone through any change or been influenced by any external forces—something that remains completely intact. Abraham the Patriarch chose to use this word for the sign that directs the Light to the entire universe. He did this in order to hint at the internal quality of that sign, thereby helping us connect to its Light and reveal it in the world.

A superficial view of the world is bound to lead us to the erroneous conclusion that the Creator intended the world to be chaotic. But *The Zohar* teaches that the entire purpose of Creation was to solve the problem of chaos—and the sign of Virgo is one of the solutions. The Creator designed the energy of Virgo to be an active channel for the revelation of Light during the month before *Rosh Hashanah*. It is, after all, a way to prepare us for the Day of Judgment— but not just for the sake of evoking regret within us over the wrongdoings of the past year. Obviously, it is not enough to say, "Sorry, I apologize for what I have done." Instead, we must accept full responsibility for our actions. None of us has the right to hurt anyone else, and certainly not because we hope that a short visit to the synagogue on *Rosh Hashanah* will wipe our slate clean. We have all come to this world in order to correct our past lives—and only by achieving this goal together can we complete our global correction.

In a previous incarnation, each one of us took less than complete advantage of the opportunity we were given to draw Light to ourselves. This time, we have come together again in order to correct this missed opportunity. We can do this by converting our desire to receive for the self alone into a desire to receive for the sake of sharing with others, out of true care and concern for our neighbors. There is no question that in order to achieve control over our destinies, we must all transform our consciousness of desire to receive for the self alone into a consciousness of sharing.

But once we have understood and accepted this idea, what are we to do? *The Zohar* tells us that when Abraham the Patriarch provided us with the cosmic calendar, he informed us that the month of *Elul* is controlled by the sign of Virgo. In practical terms, this means that the month of *Elul* provides us with the opportunity to achieve control over our lives and to shape our destinies. In this month, under the influence of Virgo, we are able literally to go back in time to those moments in which we erred and, having done so, erase those moments along with the chaos they can bring into our lives.

During *Elul*, therefore, we are able to cleanse our behaviors and return them to a virginal state. At the same time, the environment that gave rise to our past mistakes is restored to a virginal state as well. In this way, both the chaos and the setting in which that chaos took place are cleansed of all negativity. This is the full meaning of "Back to the Future"—a movie that, while generally categorized as science fiction, concerns a very practical aspect of our existence when viewed from a kabbalistic perspective.

Not only was the universe created with the capability to move forward and backward through time, but it is a *Mitzvah* to initiate this journey as part of our spiritual connection to the month of *Elul* and to the act of *Teshuvah*. Although physicists have given serious consideration to time travel over the past 100 years, Kabbalah has been familiar with that concept for more than 40 centuries. Physicists have recently speculated that under certain conditions, elementary particles might be able to travel beyond the speed of Light. The wisdom of Kabbalah explains that the keys to this process have been concealed for 2,000 years and are only now being revealed before our very eyes. But in order for us to truly make use of this wisdom, a technical understanding of *Teshuvah* is required.

We must, in short, understand the process of time travel as well as the means by which we can actualize this travel. On Shabbat, for example, we can access the time machine called *"Brich Shmei."* By means of this special excerpt from *The Zohar*, we can travel back to Mount Sinai in an instant, beyond the speed of Light. Students of Kabbalah, of course, are already familiar with this idea; we make the same journey every *Shabbat*. In the month of *Elul*, however, we make similar journeys through the power of the sign of

Virgo in order to undo our negative actions in the past. This is the only way in which we can remove the influence of such actions over our behavior in preparation for *Rosh Hashanah.* Furthermore, it is crucial that we do so, for no one in the world can avoid submitting a personal account on this Day of Judgment.

Yet even though we must submit our personal account of all our past actions on *Rosh Hashanah*, we are given a gift by special means—described by Abraham the Patriarch and explained by Rav Shimon Bar Yochai—that can enable us to correct our mistakes in advance. This is *Teshuvah*, which is not a required gesture on our part, but rather a gift—a unique opportunity to correct the historical process and to remove any aspect of chaos from the annals of the universe, as well as from our own personal lives.

Our destiny is determined by the negativity that was brought into the universe on the very day of our wrongdoing. When we remove that negativity via *Teshuvah*, the day on which the negativity was created in the past becomes a turning point for bringing positive energy to our lives. Quite literally, we have the power to go back in time and transform negative events into positive ones—to change history through the influence of thought, to remove suffering from our lives, and to balance the accounts that remain open between ourselves and others. The Creator has not abandoned or deserted us; He has given us a complete system with which we can control our destinies. And the more we understand this system, the better it will work for us.

Humanity will eventually acknowledge this wisdom, but it would certainly have benefited us all had that acknowledgment taken place 2,000 years ago. Instead, such knowledge was concealed until less than a century ago, when Rav Ashlag disclosed to us the kabbalistic wisdom hidden in *The Zohar* and the *Kitvei Ha'Ari* (the *Writings of The Ari*). Now, however, the path is open to all of mankind to go back and control the universe with peace and harmony.

With all this in mind, let us now return to the connection between the letters *Hei* and *Vav*—and, as *The Zohar* explains, in so doing find additional connections that have previously been overlooked. To offer but one example, the prospect of immortality is now being discussed as a possible reality—not just as a dream—both in scientific journals worldwide and in news media across the globe. In large part, it is genetic engineering that has lent credence to the concept of immortality. But no one stops to ask why this sudden shift in awareness is happening now. Why did it not take place 20 years ago? The truth is that these developments are clearly related to the dissemination of kabbalistic teachings and to the sudden, widespread growth in the study of Kabbalah.

When Rav Shimon said, "They brought the *Hei* back to the *Vav*," his meaning was this: "We have renewed the connection between effect and cause, between *Malchut* and *Zeir Anpin*. We have gone back to a virginal state, to the beginning, thereby revealing our true potential." As long as we did not reveal Light, the *Klipot* also had a hold on us. *Teshuvah*, however, is the most powerful means of cleansing

ourselves of negative energy, and this cleansing leads us to
the Fountain of Youth and immortality.

In the month of *Elul*, the entire universe is suffused
with Virgo consciousness to the greatest possible extent. The
power of this consciousness enables us to go back in time to
an embryonic state, to the root—to a time when we enjoyed
much more protection against negativity. An embryo's protection in the womb is far more substantial than any we are
given in the physical world.

The Rabad (Rav Abraham Ben David of Posquieres)
referred to *Elul* as "*Et Ratzon*"—"a time of goodwill." *Et
Ratzon* is the time in which the Heavenly Gates are open and
the Creator happily and lovingly receives all of us and our
prayers. But does this mean that in all other months of the
year, the Creator turns His back on us? The answer is obviously no. Kabbalah teaches that the Creator is with us every
day of the year, and that at every moment and in every month
a different aspect of His beneficence is revealed, influencing
our lives only with goodness. Yet if this is true, what point is
being made by "*Et Ratzon*" in connection with the month of
Elul?

In The Kabbalah Centre's *Siddur*, or Prayer Book, we
see that the word *ratzon* has the same numerical value, plus
one, as the מ ה ש (*Mem-Hei-Shin*), the three letter sequence
for healing from the 72 Names of God. The connection with
this Name opens a window of understanding with regard to
the month of *Elul*. In short, this month offers us the possibility

of healing both our physical and spiritual selves—and of healing others as well as the entire universe from all the ills that plague it—by means of that special aspect of the Light that is revealed only on Shabbat during the balance of the year. Kabbalistic healing differs from other healing methods in that the kabbalistic process involves going back to the root, a kind of rebirth. Yet every doctor knows that cancer begins not on the day it is diagnosed, but rather years before it first becomes manifest during an exam. In order to remove the illness, the law of cause and effect similarly requires that we go back to the day on which we caused damage to ourselves or to others.

Now we can understand how the concept of time travel enables us to realize a better future for ourselves. This realization is dependent on the removal of the negativity that we have revealed over our lifetimes, all of which has ultimately caused pain both to others and to ourselves. When we use the *Mem-Hei-Shin*, we refocus the Creator's Light, and by means of this Light we drive out the morbid darkness. This is a truly startling concept, yet there is still much more that remains to be understood.

On *Rosh Hashanah*, we connect to every aspect of the internal qualities of the month of *Elul*. In order to accomplish this, we feast together and break bread with the blessing of "*Hamotzi*" as a group. In this way, we unify our efforts and increase our chances of making the New Year the best one yet. This activity also ensures our eradication of every aspect of chaos that could plague us throughout the coming months. The only prerequisite to the success of this effort lies in our knowledge and certainty that it is in fact possible. If we lose hope and allow doubt to infuse our efforts, we will not be able to realize *Teshuvah*, use the power of *Elul*, or eliminate chaos from our midst. Mind over matter is the only rule that applies.

We will arrive at *Rosh Hashanah* with the knowledge that the New Year will be full of all the beneficence of the Light. Yet we can merit this only under the condition that we are certain of it. This is the aspect of personal accountability that Kabbalah teaches us: Each one of us is personally responsible for our own success or failure to reveal Light in our lives. There is, in short, no free ride, no matter how many other spiritual methodologies we may find. We must take this responsibility upon ourselves from the start. We must take responsibility for our negative actions and commit not to do them again—and then, with the power of our consciousness, move forward and remove every ounce of chaos from our lives in this month.

Rav Elazar's DEATH ANNIVERSARY

*W*hat does sharing mean? A person who is not busy with himself, and who is instead busy with others, is considered a sharing person. Rav Shimon and his son, Rav Elazar, knew that they had a responsibility to share with the entire world and not to give a thought to themselves. Yet they were not simply "nice people." "Nice people" who share with others are not truly sharing individuals, because the reflexive kind of sharing that they practice is their natural inclination. The righteous, by contrast, rise above their natural inclinations.

To better understand this distinction, consider what took place when Rav Shimon left the world. Rav Elazar, Rav Shimon's son, felt a sorrow that differed from what those who have lost a father or a mother ordinarily experience. The sorrow that most people feel in this situation comes from a sense of loss that is connected to the desire to receive for the self alone. A person who feels this sort of sorrow does not have the consciousness of true sharing. When a spouse dies and the surviving spouse feels sorry, this is not an expression of being true soul mates, but rather concern for the self alone.

When Rav Elazar sat with his father in a cave for 13 years, he knew it was a tremendous merit to have the obligation to undertake this task for all humanity, past, present, and future. No one was outside Rav Elazar's intention of sharing.

Whoever truly shares affects the entire world.

We must know that, at the moment we stop thinking about ourselves, we become worthy of the Light. We all came to this world with empty vessels; even a king comes into this world with empty hands. When the soul departs from this world, it goes up to the World of Truth with a sack full of good deeds in hand. And the only way to rise up to the World of Truth as thoughtful people with a sack full of good deeds is by going out of ourselves, collectively sharing with true concern for others. Yet we are all so busy looking out for ourselves that we forget how insignificant our ego needs really are.

When Rav Shimon and Rav Elazar came out of the cave after 13 years, their bodies were covered with sores. This teaches us that in order to progress and achieve something in our lives, we must first be ready to extend ourselves and experience hardship. One day Rav Elazar went to the

Upper Worlds, where he met the Angel Michael, and he asked Michael, "How do the archangels sing?" Michael answered him, "According to the *Aleph-Bet*." Consequently, all the songs that Rav Elazar wrote thereafter were written in the order of the Aramaic alphabet. The world was also created by means of the *Aleph-Bet*, and Rav Elazar's death anniversary takes place on the exact day of the creation of the world.

In the *Gemara* (an extensive commentary in Aramaic composed by the same Sages who are quoted in *The Zohar*), it is written, "Man will forever be seen as two parts: one half obligated, one half merited." Half good and half bad—that is how the entire world is constructed. Accordingly, a single Mitzvah necessitates that the entire world tilts the scales to the positive side. A single transgression tilts the scales to the negative side. This is neither an exaggeration nor a joke, but rather the truth of truths.

We are not aware of the tremendous importance of our actions, and we waste the merit and responsibility that is placed in our hands as long as we live in this world. The Maggid of Mezerich said, "The amount of Light that a person reveals is the amount manifested of his soul's power." Our Sages saw the gravity of a solitary action. Especially in the month of *Elul*, we are charged to perform every positive action possible, and it is important that each action come to fruition out of sharing consciousness—out of concern and responsibility for the destiny of the entire world. If we merit this understanding and remember it the year round, that year will be one that is changed for the better.

What is

ROSH HASHANAH?

osh Hashanah is one of the most complex and potentially transforming days of the year. Unfortunately, however, few people understand its true significance. In the portion of *Pinchas*—a section of the Torah that delineates all of the cosmic windows of the year—it is noted that *Rosh Hashanah* occurs in the seventh month, not in the first month. This is quite unexpected, as *Rosh Hashanah* is a celebration of the New Year and literally means "Head of the Year." Yet in Exodus 12, *Nissan* is designated as the year's first month. How can this seeming contradiction be resolved?

It is said that on *Rosh Hashanah* we are judged on the basis of our deeds of the past year. If we are judged in our favor —as individuals entitled to an additional chance—we will go on living for another 12 months. For many, however, living an additional year means no more than the perpetuation of suffering, pain, and disillusionment. Indeed, though the year may be seasoned with some pleasure and happiness, the prospect that all 365 days will be filled with satisfaction seems for most of us to be a remote possibility at best.

The conventional understanding of *Rosh Hashanah* is mistaken and misses the true essence of the holiday. The truth is that, for most people, the only significance of occasions such as *Rosh Hashanah* and *Pesach* are the family gatherings and festive dinners with which they are often associated. But the importance of *Rosh Hashanah* extends far beyond that of a family event. Indeed, on this day a family would be better off dispersing, for it is on *Rosh Hashanah* that Satan is granted permission to categorize any person he finds—and if an entire family is gathered together, Satan is spared the task of seeking out its individual members.

I realize that these insights contradict accepted tradition—but Kabbalah is not a tradition. Indeed, Rav Shimon Bar Yochai, the author of *The Zohar*, proposes that we abandon tradition, since it suggests a false interpretation of the Torah. And while many people have objected to the views of contemporary kabbalists, few living today would be willing to object to the opinion of Rav Shimon, whose person has been preserved for 2,000 years through the book of *The Zohar*. At its essence, therefore, *Rosh Hashanah* should be understood as anything but a family tradition or a family assembly. To the contrary, *Rosh Hashanah* is a very serious matter.

Kabbalah teaches that we are judged once a year, when we all appear before a cosmic court of justice. On this day, each person's video for the following 365 days is produced and recorded. According to Kabbalah, all of our actions are prepared and dictated to us in advance, despite our wish to see ourselves as independent and thinking human beings. To be sure, this programming can be altered, but few try to change their ways and habits—and among those who do, only a handful are able to overcome their natures and succeed. Achieving true change requires not only willpower, purpose, and perseverance, but also knowledge of how this change is to be effected. We will therefore begin here by providing knowledge of the essence of *Rosh Hashanah*.

In order to truly understand this subject, we must first raise the level of our awareness. With regard to spiritual matters, it can be said that the only way to expand our awareness is to learn and practice Kabbalah, and to read *The Zohar* and the writings of The Ari. Those who have gained high levels of awareness not only see things as they seem on the surface, but also see the concealed causes and motivating factors that cannot be revealed by our five senses alone.

So what is the purpose of *Rosh Hashanah*? Once again, it is on this day that all human beings in the world are judged. Kabbalah explains that at the Revelation on Mount Sinai, we received the message that *Rosh Hashanah* is not a day of festivity, but rather a day of judgment. The Torah, however, is not content with merely noting this troubling fact. Instead, it also provides a means of tipping the scales in our favor. Thus, *Rosh Hashanah* is transformed into a day of battle.

If during the entire year our deeds were positive, on *Rosh Hashanah* we will be guaranteed a peaceful and orderly life in the year to come. But if we have committed an unfavorable action, even inadvertently, it is possible that we will —heaven forbid—be sentenced to death during the course of the new year. It is also possible that the verdict we receive will not be so severe—but that events will take place in our lives that will disrupt our daily routine, providing us with opportunities to atone and pay for our negativities of the past year.

Therefore, the reason the Torah specifies that certain actions be taken at *Rosh Hashanah* is not in order to create a religion. Rather, these actions provide people with tools by which they may discard from their lives all disruptions and any energy of death, yielding a change for the better in the new year's script. Without these tools, we would be subject to a verdict that directly correlated with our deeds. By implementing these tools, we may find it possible to prevent the execution of our verdict, or even to fundamentally alter that verdict for the better.

Before going any further, however, we must emphasize that if the basis of *Rosh Hashanah* is the Torah—specifically in the portion of *Pinchas*—we must also understand that the Torah is actually a cosmic code. It is clear that the words of the Torah must not be taken literally—and according to Rav Shimon in the portion of *Beha'alotcha*, only a fool would do so. For if the stories of the Torah were the only things that were given on Mount Sinai, it would be possible to create a Torah that is even more amusing and interesting. Therefore, be warned that the meaning of *Rosh Hashanah*, as well as that of all other holidays, must not be taken literally; nor should all that is written about them in the Torah be interpreted in a literal sense. Rather, it should be understood that the Torah acts merely as a garment that covers the valuable cosmic code hidden within it. And it is *The Zohar* that supplies the means for understanding this cosmic code, based on the Revelation of the Torah on Mount Sinai.

Now we may prepare ourselves for a transformed perspective on the significance of *Rosh Hashanah*. According to the Talmud, all nations of the world—not only the Israelites—are judged on this holiday, which is also called the Day of Judgment. But why was this specific day chosen? Not merely because it is written. The effect does not create the cause; it can clarify that cause but can never determine it. Thus, if we are discussing times and dates, we cannot understand the cause without first considering the astrological aspects of the Torah's time schedule.

The purpose of the Torah's time schedule is to give mankind some insight into cosmic activity. Our purpose in studying this is not to examine the physics of space as conventional space research programs might do, but rather to investigate the inner intelligence of these heavenly bodies. This, in essence, is kabbalistic astrology. Without an understanding of kabbalistic astrology, we cannot even begin to understand the meaning of *Rosh Hashanah*. Even with all the wisdom contained in the Talmud, we would be dealing only with a superficial religious model were it not for kabbalistic astrology. Within the Torah there is a code, the solution of which has eluded us for 2,000 years.

Why does *Rosh Hashanah* occur exactly when it does? In *The Zohar*, the portion of *Pinchas* refers to a verse in the Torah (Numbers 29:1): "And in the seventh month, on the first day of the month." This refers to *Tishrei*, the sign of Libra. This verse leads us to conclude that the first month is *Nissan*, the sign of Aries, as the Book of Exodus makes clear: "This month (*Nissan*) shall be unto you the beginning of months."

But by the Gregorian calendar, January is the first month of the year. So why don't we celebrate the New Year on the first day of *Tishrei*? In fact, *Rosh Hashanah* is not called a holiday at all. There are only three basic holidays, and *Rosh Hashanah* is not among them. On January 1, the world celebrates the beginning of a new year. But the first day of *Tishrei* belongs to a different category altogether. On this day, rather than celebrating, we go to synagogue and pray, for in fact this is not the beginning of the year. Still, we greet each other with "*Shanah Tovah*," or Happy New Year.

This raises some perplexing questions. Even The Ari inquires, "When was the universe created: in *Tishrei* or in *Nissan*, on *Rosh Hashanah* or right before *Pesach*?" The Talmud also occupies a good deal of text dealing with the matter.

For comparison, let us look at another important question: Why should the Land of Israel belong to the Israelites? According to Rav Isaac Luria, Israel belongs to the Israelites because the Creator promised it to them. The King of Persia, the King of Babylonia, the King of Greece, and the Roman Emperor, each of whom ruled the world at one time or another—all sought to conquer Israel, especially Jerusalem. But why? What lies in this small region of land that could possibly be of such consequence? Kabbalah, of course, provides the answer: Israel is the center of energy for the entire world.

In order to maintain the world in a balanced manner, there must be one group that possesses the knowledge to maintain the structure and order of the universe—and this is the People of Israel. The Israelites control and maintain a structure of continuity, certainty, and peace on earth, preventing chaos, destruction, and ruin. Yet despite all the knowledge that has been in their possession, the Israelites have not been able to fully actualize that knowledge. In much the same manner, one may have a theoretical understanding of how to manufacture an automobile, but nothing can come of it unless there are machines to carry out the work, factories to house the machines, and workers to operate them.

Consider this: We do not know what the Creator looks like, nor do we know what He is made of, or anything tangible about Him. All we know is that the power of God exists, that it is expressed through a force called the Light, and that Light is the energy that rules the world. When Rav Isaac

Luria discusses the giving of Israel to the Israelites, he says that the knowledge that will eventually be received by the Israelites will have to be received in the Land of Israel. From this place—from Israel—the people of Israel will draw the power to rule the world. When other nations claim that we have taken Israel from them, the answer will be that non-Israelites have never been privy to this knowledge. Even when they have physically conquered Israel, they have gained control only over a physical piece of land that in itself is no more significant than Madagascar.

When the proper spiritual work was performed in the Land of Israel, as was the case during the time of King Solomon, there was peace throughout the entire world—for King Solomon used the very same code we use to bless the new moon. But when the Israelites lost the knowledge they possessed or chose not to implement it, they also lost their right to dwell in Israel and were dispersed to all corners of the earth. The Creator promised Israel to the Israelites on the condition that they serve—with the help of the knowledge given to them—as channels for the revelation of the Light in the world in a balanced and harmonious way, as specified by the first Mitzvah mentioned by the Torah (*Kiddush HaLevanah*, the Sanctification of the New Moon).

Without this spiritual work, it makes no difference whether the Israelites are in Israel or anywhere else. Therefore, it is written in Genesis that Israel is the place from which peace may be maintained in the world, just as it came to be in the days of King Solomon. But when the

Israelites do not understand what their true purpose in Israel is, they have no right to the land. We have not received Israel because we are Israelites, but rather because we have received the knowledge and the spiritual tools required for the realization of Israel's potential.

With this understanding, we can now investigate what really took place when the world was created. So what is the significance of the world having been created in *Nissan* as opposed to its having been created in *Tishrei*? The land, and with it Israel as the energy center of the world, was created on the third day of Creation. But what is creation? This is precisely the point of the discussion. Creation can, from a limited perspective, describe the establishment of a business. Only after a business is established can income be created. But is this always the case? The answer is no. The mere existence of a plan does not imply its realization. There are cosmic influences that come into play as well, as explained in the book *Star Connection*.

When Rav Joshua said that the world was created in the month of *Nissan*, what he meant to say was that even though the world was in its place in the month of *Tishrei*—the land was created in *Tishrei*, and the center of energy was ready in *Tishrei*—only in the month of *Nissan* was it activated, and only then did it realize its previously dormant potential. Only in the month of *Nissan* was the energy center first used, and only then did the world receive understanding and consciousness.

Rav Joshua raised the issue of when the world was created, but he meant to ask different questions: "When did the world begin to be creative? When did we begin to control our own destinies and cease to be robots?" Genesis 2:20 says that after the creation of the first man, ". . . man gave names to all cattle, and to the fowl of the air." *The Zohar* says not only that man gave names to all the creatures, but that when those names were given, the creatures became animated for the first time. Only then did the grass began to grow and the animals begin to move.

In view of all this, when was the world really created? Was it when everything was ready but frozen, or when everything began to live? This concept can be likened to a man who constructs a shoe manufacturing plant. The production line is ready, and all the machines and raw materials are in place, but the plant does not produce a thing. This is because the potential exists but has not yet been realized. Taking this example one step further, one might conclude that what Rav Joshua meant to say was that in the month of *Nissan*, the plant began to manufacture shoes. Until *Nissan*, in other words, the world was in robotic consciousness. All our lives were but a playback of prerecorded cassettes, void of consciousness. Exodus was not only a departure from this lack of consciousness, but also a departure from a state of slavery to a new state of consciousness—a state of liberty, of true free choice, an ascent above the influence of the planets to a control over destiny. Therefore, there is no connection between the Exodus as understood by the kabbalists and the historic event of the Exodus as celebrated by Israelites throughout the generations. When Americans celebrate the Fourth of July, they are celebrating a tradition. When we celebrate *Pesach*, we are celebrating the beginning of creativity in the world. Yet for those who have not connected to the instruments of controlled destiny, *Pesach*, the day before, and the day after are all indistinguishable.

Preparations for Rosh Hashanah

The *Shofar* (or ram's horn), our main tool on *Rosh Hashanah*, is not just a "tradition." Before blowing it, we say ("happy are the people who know *T'ruah*") because knowledge equals connection. Without the knowledge—without the connection to the quantum—it is as if we have not changed a thing over the past 2,000 years. *Rosh Hashanah* is the day in which we may return to the future, or return to Adam's first day of existence before the Sin—but this time without repeating his historic mistake.

As we discussed earlier, the meaning of *Teshuvah* is much more profound than simply saying, "I'm sorry." *Teshuvah*, true repentance, means going back to a point prior to our having committed a transgression and, having done so, reverse the scene so that it is as though that transgression never took place. Put another way, it means that we must go back in time.

Teshuvah means an actual return in time and a rectification at the core of that which is distorted. Even if a man has committed a murder, he may go back in time, choose not to murder, and revive his victim. Any manifestation of negativity in the area of awareness of the Tree of Knowledge of Good and Evil, including manifestations of violence such as murder or theft, may be canceled by transferring the awareness from the physical level to the highest spiritual level—to the World of Truth, to the Tree of Life, to a world of certainty, order, harmony, and absolute positivity.

Since murder is part of the existence of the physical universe, it too is included among the matters that can be controlled. Murder is merely a physical action, as the soul does not die as a result of it but merely separates from the physical body. Thus, if a person were to use the tools described by The Ari in his book *Gates of Meditations*, it would indeed be possible to revive a murder victim. Specifically, if the murderer performed the act of true *Teshuvah* on *Rosh Hashanah*—or at another appropriate time, as determined by the Creator—the soul of the victim would on that day be impregnated in a fertilized egg, and a pregnancy would begin that would bring the murdered person to life in a new incarnation. This rectification does not apply only to a murderer who kills and then repents in this generation (or reincarnation); one may also repent for an act of murder committed in a previous generation.

By performing the act of *Teshuvah*, we have the ability to create a body for the murder victim's soul. In order to achieve this purification, however, we must honestly say to ourselves: I wish to change the desire to receive for myself alone, which caused me to commit the transgressions against another human being and not against the Creator.

Is the Creator influenced by our actions? No, He is not. The issue here is the negative consciousness that has been injected into the universe as a result of our misdeeds. It must be understood that good people may also be affected by the negative energy that we have created. We are discussing two types of transgressions: those directed toward others, and those directed toward the Creator. "The Creator" refers here to the entire universe that reflects and represents Him. One must change the desire to receive, return in time, disappear, and enter the parallel universe because each sin committed begins with the innate properties of the human activity—that is, the desire to receive for the self alone.

Technology
(Prayer/Shofar/Meditation)

Let us now turn to a discussion of the technologies and weapons that we may use at *Rosh Hashanah*. Here we are engaged in a battle over metaphysical issues. The forces we will send to the front depend on the knowledge we possess; knowledge is the connection, and knowledge is the stockpile of weapons we will need in order to fight the battle. And reading *The Zohar*, or even only scanning the Aramaic letters, can prepare us for this battlefield, thereby ensuring the success of our efforts.

Using the sound of the *Shofar* is like activating a remote control that is intended to awaken something supernal. But what is supernal? Is it that which lies beyond human perception? In order to awaken "above," we must also awaken "'below" by means of a physical instrument that will connect us to the supernal instrument. Yet in doing so, one cannot use just any instrument; one must know precisely which instrument to use in order to get to the right place.

The Aramaic word שׁוֹפָר (*Shofar*) has the numerical value of 586. Was it coincidental that the ram's horn was given the name "*Shofar?*" Certainly not. To the contrary, it is a code to help us understand the energetic essence of the physical material known as a ram's horn.

The Zohar emphasizes the utmost importance of blowing the *Shofar* using the correct technique and the correct meditations. This is because the *Shofar* is our means of entering into the universe and of turning a field of ruin into a place of peace and quiet. The physical blowing itself, according to *The Zohar*, is not sufficient. If it is not accompanied by the right meditations, the blowing will indeed create a communication system, but that system will be of no use to us. Instead, it will be like a network of telephones and cables that, while in perfect working order, remains void of all content because it is not being used to transmit ideas.

The word *Shofar* and the word *takfu* (meaning "they attacked") have the same numerical value. Since the two words have a common denominator, valuable information may be obtained from them. The meaning of the term *takfu* is to fight against, to penetrate, even to cancel and erase. The *Shofar*, because of its numerical value, introduces us to the instrument that will perform the task of canceling and erasing the desire to receive for the self alone—a desire that we ourselves created. We must therefore recognize that the *Shofar*, the physical instrument, has the ability to establish a direct channel of communication with the inner stratum of the universe, the cosmic court of justice—as well as to destroy, using the system of blowing, the prosecution case that Satan intends to file against us.

The use of the *Shofar* involves three aspects—as does the *Machzor* (Holiday Prayer Book), which is similarly constructed according to the "aspect of three." The *Shofar's* first blowing takes place before the *Musaf* (additional) *Amidah* prayer. Here the Sages formulated three blessings: one each for the right, left, and central columns. And in this context it is important not only to know exactly what this means, but also to understand that without the correct meditation and the appropriate intention, the spiritual work cannot be performed.

It is the good fortune of Israel as well as the whole world that the Sages formed the connection between right, left, and central columns, and that they manifested this connection in a physical manner. Abraham, Isaac, and Jacob were the missing links between the physical and the metaphysical. Therefore, although all the forms of thought were created during the first three days of Creation as described in Genesis 1, mankind could not use this power for their daily needs as long as the energy did not materialize as Abraham, Isaac, and Jacob. These three Chariots enable the entire world to connect with the Light. And when this universal connection takes place, peace and brotherhood reign.

We must go back to the moment before the Sin of Adam and make the necessary correction. And this is what we do together on *Rosh Hashanah*—because we all want a good year, and we know that the power to bring that about is in our hands.

Yet a good year does not come about without effort, and effort does not just lie in hearing the *Shofar*. To the contrary, we must return in time—and perform the act of *Teshuvah*—through the methodology of *The Zohar*.

This return in time is accomplished through the recitation of Brich Shmae. Of course, anyone who recites Brich Shmae without knowing its purpose achieves nothing. As more and more people recite Brich Shmae with the correct intention, however, we will succeed in drawing closer—and ultimately returning—to the state of Adam before the Sin.

Our purpose here is to recover something that was lost—to return to a part of ourselves that we once had without knowing it, that we lost without knowing just what we had lost or when. Now we can gain access to something more than our everyday human potential. We can connect with our true inner selves, and forming that connection will also enable us to relate to the inner stratum of the universe.

Prayers and meditations do not inherently have the power to elevate physicality to a spiritual level; they merely have the power to connect our subconscious with the spiritual world. Nothing is revealed in the physical world by prayer itself. Prayer does not deal with the dimension of *Malchut*, with total revelation in the material realm. Thus, The Ari has written that prayer or meditation cannot lead to results in the corporeal or physical dimension.

The human soul has the potential to achieve a higher level of awareness than that of angels. It is true that angels are not limited by physical reality; they can indeed move through doors and walls, and can instantly move from any location to another. Yet at the same time, angels are unable to ascend to the Worlds of *Yetzirah* (Formation), *Briyah* (Creation), or *Atzilut* (Emanation). An angel is an entity or power that serves as a metaphysical channel for the conduction of Light, just as radio waves transmit messages. Therefore, each task in the world has a specific angel, and each prayer has an angel whose job is to elevate and transmit it.

The reasons for prayer and meditation are explained by *The Zohar*. From a kabbalistic standpoint, the internal reality of a stone, of a person, and of the entire universe is one unified whole. If together we can transform the different manifestations of this internal reality into one, we will be able to control everything in the universe. Humanity has been given this responsibility and authority. Both in meditation and in prayer, we must break free of the illusions of the material dimension and establish a direct connection between ourselves and the entire universe. And while this is not a simple task, it is an essential one. According to *The Zohar*, if we make this cosmic connection—which is really a connection to ourselves, since everything is one unified whole—the world will be filled with the peace and tranquillity we so desperately seek. But if we do not do so, we can only return to chaos.

The people of the world have yet to understand the connection that we are describing here. Eventually, however, this great unification will occur, and chaos will simply pass from existence. When we learn to communicate with our true inner selves, the result will be revolutionary. Yet in truth, we have no alternative but to undertake this task, for neither science nor any other institution can guarantee us that "tomorrow will be a better day." And while there have indeed been moments of tranquillity in our lives, not one person today remains unaffected by the chaos that pervades our world. Every effort must therefore be made to diminish the negative energy in the universe, which is the real cause of chaos.

In essence, we need to project ourselves to a dimension in which our physical bodies—the cause of all problems—do not exist. And to bring this about, let us begin with the first aspect of meditation. The Aramaic letter פ (*Pei*) connects us to Venus, which rules the astrological sign of Libra. According to *The Zohar*, when we connect with the *Pei* through meditation, we are in fact connecting with the hierarchy of the universe and of ourselves. The letter ל (*Lamed*) created Libra, and together with Venus it rules the internal and external influences of this month. When we meditate on the *Pei* and on the *Lamed* in this place, we form a connection with the entire universe. Yet we must make a conscious effort to remove all negative aspects of Venus and Libra and to connect only to their positive aspects.

After meditating with this intention for a moment or two, we continue with the prayer that is said before the blessings that precede the *Shofar* blowing. At the same time, we must understand that the words of the prayers are only channels. According to The Ari, meditation, or guided thought, is the most important part of the prayer.

The prayer begins with "from the suffering I called, O God" (Tehilim 118:5). Through this combination we will succeed in performing "the tearing of Satan." In essence, we tear away the negative energy of the desire to receive for the self alone. We prepare our communications cable with the goal of eradicating the desire to receive for the self alone that we created during the past year. The intent of the prayer must be such that the desire to receive for self alone will not be a part of our lives.

After finishing this prayer, we are ready for the blessings. The first is this: "Blessed are you Hashem, our God, King of the World, Who sanctified us with His commandments and commanded us the hearing of the sound of the *Shofar*."

But what is meant by "Blessed are you"? The conventional interpretation of this phrase is incorrect. The Creator, after all, has no need of any blessing on our part, for He is not lacking anything; only the desire to receive for the self alone can include lack. The blessing just recited should thus be seen simply as a link—a channel to the *Shofar* itself. The blessing is, in essence, like dialing a telephone—but at the same time, it is something very different. Although the *Shofar* is a physical object, we connect not to the material aspect of the instrument but rather to the inner voice that comes from within it. Our thought consciousness connects with the sound of the *Shofar*, which acts as a channel and brings our thoughts to their destination. This is because the power of this sound can, according to *The Zohar*, reach every universe and galaxy that was, will be, or can ever be conceived. And when we feed the correct thought and intention into the channel of sound, we make the cosmic connection that is the essence of prayer.

Kabbalah teaches that hearing the sound of the *Shofar* creates connection between our ears and the "supreme ear," which is *Binah*, the energy storehouse of Light. Therefore the fitting word is *lishmo'ah* (to hear), to form the ear-to-ear connection. We devote only two days of our lives to this effort, yet these are two days that can, according to Kabbalah, result in a good year without the disadvantages that otherwise accompany all human behavior. *Binah* is associated with Libra, the scales— and when the scales are tipped in our favor, the Light will lead us in the coming year.

The second blessing is this: "Blessed are you Hashem, our God, King of the World who has kept us alive, sustained us, and brought us to this time."

This blessing has three stages that correlate with the consciousness of the atom (right, left, and central)—the desire to share, the desire to receive (i.e., energy that is negative but nevertheless vital to the creation of the cycle), and the central force of resistance. Before giving a detailed description of the stages, however, we will note that the phrase "given us life" refers to the right column; "sustenance" to the left column; and "brought us" to the central column. We should also be aware that on the first day of *Rosh Hashanah*, we are concerned with serious transgressions of the desire to receive for ourselves. These are expressed as *dinah kashiah*, meaning strong or harsh judgment. On this day, all of our efforts will be directed toward destroying that form of negativity.

The second day of *Rosh Hashanah* is concerned with less serious transgressions, expressed as *dinah rafiah*, signifying weak or soft judgment. Perhaps one might think that our attack on Satan during the second day might require a less powerful intention. But we must not relax our pressure and effort at this time and must instead continue as before, for in the war against Satan there is not a single insignificant moment. As long as the enemy has not been completely destroyed—"and death destroyed forever" (Yeshayah 25:8)—the danger we face will persist.

Two words—*T'ruah* (blast) and *Shevarim* (breaks)— describe our two forms of attack. *Shevarim* is an offensive against the harsh judgments, while *T'ruah* concerns the soft judgments. One might ask why we are also concerned with the attack on the soft judgments on the first day. The answer is this: Our Sages understood that man cannot precisely distinguish the various types of transgressions. The theft of a large amount of money from a bank, for example, might well create less suffering for the victim than that caused by a theft which, although seemingly insignificant, represents the sole income of a man of limited means.

Through *The Zohar*, we connect to balance. *The Zohar* teaches that when our spiritual missiles are launched, they receive a push from our Forefathers to the next stage and eventually come to rest in Jacob's tent. This happens when our spiritual missiles arrive at the *Sfirah* of *Tiferet*, which is the central column. What is the significance of this? We must understand that the missiles we launch are "anti-missile missiles." In yet another sense, they are a vaccine. A vaccine takes a live virus and connects it with the antivirus, its opposite.

The spiritual virus of Satan's awareness is surrounded during the *Teki'ot* (soundings) of the *Shofar* and is encircled by two aspects. It is surrounded first by the channel of *Chesed*, the positive energy channel, and then by the channel of the central column, which is *Tiferet*. When these two forces join together, they have the power to destroy any spiritual virus. More precisely, we have taken the energy of the virus and weakened it; after which, we inject the weakened virus into our bodies. There the weakened, injected virus subdues the virus itself, which now has positive consciousness as well.

The secret of this vaccine is found in *The Zohar*. In order to subdue the negative energy of the desire to receive for the self alone—that energy which prevents us from receiving from the energy storehouse—we must take the desire to receive for the self alone and turn it into a vaccine. And from the moment we succeed in creating such a vaccine, we launch the anti-missile missiles toward the desire to receive for the self alone. It's an exciting battle—a sort of "Star Wars" that takes place every year. And according to *The Zohar*, happy are those who can stand up to the missile of negativity and destroy it!

This anti-missile can also benefit people who are in for an "accident" or misfortune in their lives but have no idea that it is related to their negative activity. Such people need a dose of energy for an additional year. The negative consciousness created as a result of their actions will determine whether the missile of negativity will bring death or, alternatively, whether it will bring about only a year of intense suffering. At *Rosh Hashanah*, we must construct the hardware and software that will bring about the best possible outcome.

The hardware referred to above is the power of the Light that will destroy any missile of the desire to receive for the self alone. What is meant in *The Zohar* by *chazek yadai* (strengthen my hands)? It simply means that there is no coercion involved in spirituality. If mankind does not create the appropriate channels for the force of Creation, the Light will not be revealed. This is what the Creator is waiting for on *Rosh Hashanah*: chazek yadi, or "seat Me on the throne"—because on this specific day, the missiles come to inject us with negative energy that can bring suffering worse than death.

The software cited above consists of three groups of spiritual missiles. The first group contains the energy of the right column. This group, which will be referred to as Abraham, represents the desire to share. This aspect of the software comes into being immediately after the two blessings and before the *Amidah*, the *Shemoneh Esrei*, the most important part of each prayer during the year. The second group is the energy of the desire to receive, which is negative thought consciousness and connects us with the energy of Isaac. This aspect of the software is activated during the *Amidah* service, when the entire congregation stands in silence and quietly recites the group of the left column. The last group, the final disk of the software, will be guided by the energy of the central column which connect us to the energy of Jacob. The construction of the third group of software takes place when the *Amidah* service is repeated—the Repetition by the prayer leader. By repeating the *Amidah*, we construct the final file, which is the desire to receive for the sake of sharing.

Preceding these blessings is an additional prayer—one that creates a kind of insulation for the *Shofar*. We need such insulation because on this day, all negative energy missiles are set for an attack. To help us ensure the protection of our chief weapon, the *Shofar's* anti-missile Laser beam, there is a prayer in the book taken from Psalm 47 that is repeated seven times. But we must be aware that the power of the prayer lies not in its words, which are secondary, but rather in the intention. Before the first reading of the prayer, the words must be consciously injected with awareness of *Chesed*. As was mentioned, the Sfirot are a form of stored metaphysical energy, and this is exactly what we need to protect the *Shofar's* offensive from Satan's thought consciousness. But why is the prayer repeated seven times? The answer is that the readings establish communication. And the beam emitted from the *Shofar*, carrying the guided thought with it, forms the essence of this communication.

It should be understood that the laser beam to which we are referring is a visual metaphor only. In point of fact, the power of the *Shofar's* sound is far greater than that of any laser beam, no matter how powerful it may be. But we must inject guided thought into this beam. With each reading of the prayer, we aim at the internal energy of the following Sfirot: *Gvurah*,

Tiferet, Netzach, Hod, and *Yesod.* And on the seventh reading, we inject the thought consciousness of *Malchut.*

Each blowing of the *Shofar* must be very precise, and each must produce a particular sound. Before the beam is launched, it must also be injected with the correct meditation. If this seems complicated, remember that this issue is literally a matter of life and death, and one that therefore demands great effort. Only people who understand this matter have any business being in the war room. (You can't win a battle if you don't really understand why you are there.)

So how do the different beams sound, and how is each of them distinctive? (Remember, earlier we said that *T'ruah* means "blast" and *Shevarim* means "breaks," while *Teki'ot* are "soundings.") The *T'kiah* is one long blast, while the *T'ruah* is a series of at least nine short, sharp, penetrating blows. The *Shevarim* constitute three longer blowings. The nine blowings (of *T'ruah*) are grouped together in groups of three, and each group sounds as one. The length of the *Shevarim* is approximately that of the *T'ruah.* The sounds are delivered in respective cycles, described in detail. The final *T'kiah* in a cycle is delivered as one long, continuous blow that lasts, at a minimum, for a time equal to nine short blowings.

In the prayer book, we find a combination of different frames of reference. As mentioned, the first set of the prayer has three parts. This is the set that is attributed to Abraham's frame of reference—the right column. When the blessings are heard, this is the signal to build the frame of reference for the specific reading of the prayer, which contains three parts. Here, too, it is clear that the number three refers to the three components of any frame of reference: right column of right column, left column of right column, and central column of right column, respectively. We create three smaller frames of reference, and in this way we conceive both the unity of the entire frame and its division into parts as being Abraham. Each part of the first set is subdivided into three stages as well. The technology of the offensive, therefore, is very precise. Science cannot fathom how thought consciousness can travel distances of billions of light years, yet in fact, the distance does not exist; it is an illusion. On *Rosh Hashanah*, we have the good fortune to receive futuristic energy that can be used for the reduction of judgments and for the control of our destiny.

In fact, we are the ones who make our minds think. In the everyday world, television and computers seem to be usurping our power of thought. But suddenly, at least on *Rosh Hashanah*, we are supposed to use our own minds as computers. This may sound strange to the vast majority of the world's inhabitants, but it is a fine time to begin—for *Rosh Hashanah* is not merely an exercise in the development of the mind computer, but rather an exercise in life itself. If all that has been said here is true, and if there is no coercion involved in spirituality, then we must search within ourselves and ask, "Is it worth it?" My intention here is only to share the knowledge of the kabbalists, who claim that we have the technology to create the DNA, both physical and metaphysical, with which to transform creation. To be sure, this notion may seem strange in the beginning; perhaps we must strain our mental powers, which may be rusty, in order to comprehend it. But if we do so, the rust will eventually erode, and we may then discover a whole world—one that our minds did not previously have the ability to perceive.

Before blowing the *Shofar*, we construct an Abraham right column (the first set), which has three parts: the first, "right" (Abraham); the second, "left" (Isaac); and the third, "'central" (Jacob). As was mentioned previously, each part is additionally divided into three stages. This is true for the other two sets as well. Therefore, if we understand one set, we know all that needs to be known about the blowing of the *Shofar*. The division of the parts into stages also runs parallel to the right-column energy, the left-column energy, and the energy of the central column. Each section is in turn broken into its own sets, parts, and stages.

ROSH HASHANAH T'KIOT (SHOFAR BLOWING) MEDITATION

AVRAHAM - IDOL WORSHIPPING			
RIGHT	RIGHT T'ki'a Shevarim T'ruah T'ki'a	LEFT T'ki'a Shevarim T'ruah T'ki'a	CENTRAL T'ki'a Shevarim T'ruah T'ki'a
LEFT	RIGHT T'ki'a Shevarim T'ki'a	LEFT T'ki'a Shevarim T'ki'a	CENTRAL T'ki'a Shevarim T'ki'a
CENTER	RIGHT T'ki'a T'ruah T'ki'a	LEFT T'ki'a T'ruah T'ki'a	CENTRAL T'ki'a T'ruah T'ki'a Gdolah

YITZCHAK - INCEST			
RIGHT	RIGHT T'ki'a Shevarim T'ruah T'ki'a	LEFT T'ki'a Shevarim T'ki'a	CENTRAL T'ki'a T'ruah T'ki'a
LEFT	RIGHT T'ki'a Shevarim T'ruah T'ki'a	LEFT T'ki'a Shevarim T'ki'a	CENTRAL T'ki'a T'ruah T'ki'a
CENTER	RIGHT T'ki'a Shevarim T'ruah T'ki'a	LEFT T'ki'a Shevarim T'ki'a	CENTRAL T'ki'a T'ruah T'ki'a Gdolah

YA'AKOV - BLOODSHED			
RIGHT	RIGHT T'ki'a Shevarim T'ruah T'ki'a	LEFT T'ki'a Shevarim T'ki'a	CENTRAL T'ki'a T'ruah T'ki'a
LEFT	RIGHT T'ki'a Shevarim T'ruah T'ki'a	LEFT T'ki'a Shevarim T'ki'a	CENTRAL T'ki'a T'ruah T'ki'a
CENTER	RIGHT T'ki'a Shevarim T'ruah T'ki'a	LEFT T'ki'a Shevarim T'ki'a	CENTRAL T'ki'a T'ruah T'ki'a Gdolah

DAVID - EVIL SPEEACH	
RIGHT	T'ki'a Shevarim T'ruah T'ki'a
LEFT	T'ki'a Shevarim T'ki'a
CENTER	T'ki'a T'ruah T'ki'a Gdolah

The first part of the set of Abraham is *T'kiah-Shevarim-T'ruah-T'kiah*. This cycle of four blows of the *Shofar* is repeated three times. The four blows always appear together in the first part of the set, and the right column is the focus. Within each part, we can discern the stages. For example, let us take the second stage of the first part of the first set. When we are ready for the second stage of *T'kiah-Shevarim-T'ruah-T'kiah*, before the initial *T'kiah* we must inject the frame of reference of the second stage of the first part of the first set, which is "left column of right column of right column."

Now we arrive at the actual launching of sounds. First we have determined the frame of reference, and this is the intention. Without the intention, nothing is achieved. The intention injects the specific awareness, which is the spiritual channel of communication—a nonmaterial, wireless channel. And this is the consciousness that will meet the weapon that is coming to attack us on *Rosh Hashanah*. On that day we will also ask for energy from the energy storehouse. Perhaps we might not be aware of all of these processes, but our soul has submitted the request to the energy storehouse. And when this request is submitted, if at some time during the year we also construct a satanic energy missile made of the desire to receive for the self alone, our request cannot and will not arrive at its destination. According to Kabbalah, this missile of desire to receive will most certainly intercept our request.

Let us now return to the second stage of the first part of the first set. Before the blowing of the *Shofar*, the thought must be injected into the left-column stage of the right-column set. But our minds must work quickly here, as this thought should occur during the split second just before the blowing. Does this process take a long time? In a regular synagogue, the first set takes 10 minutes. At The Kabbalah Centre, it takes 30 minutes or more, for the negative energy is very strong on this day, and it really seeks to crash our computer. Occasionally that negative energy does succeed, in which case the mental process must be repeated until all negative thoughts have been canceled. Satan is there—do not be mistaken. Give him the opportunity to jam your computer, and when he thinks he has succeeded, sneak up on him again and do not proceed until you have injected the correct thought that must come prior to the blowing itself.

Those who feel they cannot keep track of the meditations in their minds can, upon initiation of the *T'kiah*, rely on their earlier construction—on the thought consciousness of the specific set and the specific part. In such a case, during the blowing of the *Shofar*, one need think only of the following: The right column governs the *T'kiah*, the left column governs both the *Shevarim* and the *T'ruah*, and the central column governs the last *T'kiah* in a cycle of soundings.

But why two left columns? It is for the same reason that *Rosh Hashanah* lasts for two days. The kabbalists' response is that this refers to the distinction between the two kinds of transgressions: harsh judgments and soft judgments. The *Shevarim* are directed at harsh judgments and the *T'ruah* at soft judgments.

Shevarim and *T'ruah* are both connected to the negative energy of the left column—that is, to Isaac. The *Shevarim*, as mentioned, are composed of three *Teki'ot*, and the *T'ruah* of nine short *Teki'ot*. The *Shevarim* are connected to extremely negative human activity, while the *T'ruah*, *Malchut*, counteracts lighter transgressions. In *Shevarim* we inject the energetic thought of *Gvurah*. Meditating on the word *Gvurah* during the *Shevarim* and on the word *Malchut* during the *T'ruah* will suffice for us to construct our anti-missile missile.

Let us reiterate: In the first *T'kiah*, the injection is of the thought of the right column, or Abraham. In *Shevarim*, the injection is *Gvurah*, or the word Isaac. In *T'ruah*, it is the word *Malchut*, or the word David. On the last *T'kiah*, the intention we think about is Jacob, or the central column. The technique is simple; this is all that is needed. We will also note that the same intention is injected into the first part of the next two sets, respectively.

We now turn to the second part of the first set. This is the part of the left column. Here, the order of *Shofar* blowings is *T'kiah-Shevarim-T'kiah*. The first *T'kiah* is the right column; the *Shevarim*, the left column; and the final *T'kiah*, the central column.

The third part of the first set is composed of *T'kiah-T'ruah-T'kiah*. The *T'ruah* is *Malchut*, the negative energy, but to a lesser extent than in *Shevarim*. In the third stage of the third part of the first blowing, we will notice the phrase *T'kiah Gedolah* (Great *T'kiah*). The kabbalists realized that when the final *T'kiah* is completed, for some metaphysical reason the manifestation of the central column that occurs at this stage holds major significance within the entire technology. That is why we extend the last *T'kiah* as long as possible, or as long as the person blowing the *Shofar* is able.

We now proceed to the *Amidah* prayer. We will again see the use of the *Shofar* in three different places, but here there is a difference. In the *Amidah*, it is no longer required that there be three series of blowings; rather, one series in each part is sufficient. This is the main difference between the first set and the second and third sets. In the *Amidah* prayer, which is recited silently by the congregation, we refer to the negative energy of the left column—or Isaac—in this, the second of the sets. This set is to be injected with the same guiding thoughts as those we have learned for the first set; its method is identical. Nevertheless, in contrast to the set of Abraham—a set in which there are three different parts, each divided into three different stages—the parts in the set of Isaac are not divided into stages. Instead, all parts are identical.

In the third set (which is the repetition of the *Amidah*), we inject the meditation on Jacob, or the central column, before beginning the first part. We then continue to the second part, which is the left column, and then the third, which is the central column. This set is not subdivided into stages, and with that we have nearly completed the three sets of stages required for our attack on the missiles of negative energy. Nevertheless, at the end of the repetition of the *Amidah*, there is an additional set that is connected to *Malchut*. The structure here is similar to the parts and stages of the second and third sets, but with one principal difference. While the second and third sets each have three parts, *Malchut*—the fourth set—has only one series of blowings: *T'kiah-T'ruah-T'kiah*. In this set—which is connected to *Malchut*, the desire to receive—we recite the *Kaddish* prayer.

Why do the *T'kiah*, the *T'ruah*, and the *Shevarim* sound the way they do? There is a *T'kiah* of the right column and a *T'kiah* of the central column. These are positive energies, so there are no interruptions or fragmentations—for as in life, fragmentation and separation exist only in negativity. If something is positive, then it has a smooth flow of energy. Therefore, the *T'kiah* is one long sound. The *Shevarim* and the *T'ruah* are fragmented because they are connected to negative energy. The word *Shevarim* comes from the Aramaic word *shever*, to break. *T'ruah* is similarly a form of cutting or separation.

Through this simple knowledge, we become captains of our own ships, and by that means the most profound secrets of the Kabbalah are revealed to us. This has never happened before, but it is happening now. In the Book of Jeremiah, proof is found that in this, the Age of Aquarius, we will reap benefits that no generation before us could ever have hoped to receive. In Jeremiah 31:33 it is written, "And they shall teach no more every man his neighbor, and every man his brother, saying: 'Know Hashem.'" In other words, there will be no need for spiritual coercion, and there will be no need for people to be taught. Everyone will know God, and everyone will know the power of the Light: "For they shall all know Me, from the least of them unto the greatest of them, said Hashem; for I will forgive their iniquity, and their sin will I remember no more."

This passage does indeed have a visionary sound, but consider the fact that in a very short time we have learned how to defend ourselves in the event of Star Wars—or, as *The Bible* calls it, the war of *Gog* and *Magog*, the ultimate war. In Aramaic, the words *Gog* and *Magog* (the Armageddon war) are derived from the word *hagigim*, or thoughts, and imply the power of thought. The artillery used in this battle will be the human mind. With the power of thought, we can learn to defend ourselves. And it is here that the kabbalists are several steps ahead of the scientific community, for science has yet to make its final leap onto the metaphysical plane. If the method presented here seems complicated, review it and you will be surprised to discover just how much you have learned.

The process of this computerized meditation will bring with it many side benefits. The world around you, for example, will suddenly be seen from a different angle, and you will have infinitely greater awareness. Things you have never seen before will suddenly be visible, as if they had not previously existed.

You cannot know how effective things are until you try. We're lucky because we can say: We can prevent a holocaust by preventing Satan—the negative consciousness—from gaining control. According to kabbalistic thought, the armament that will be used in the coming war will not be laser beams, but rather thought consciousness. But perhaps one might wonder if the dissemination of such powerful information might cause damage. The answer is that even if one understands the entire knowledge of the Kabbalah, this information cannot be used unless the user has a consciousness of "love your neighbor as yourself." For this reason, it cannot possibly fall into the wrong hands.

Using this powerful technology, we can erase flaws, tragedies, and catastrophes from the scripts of our lives. We are no longer fated to experience each day as something that lies far beyond our control. At one point this was the only route available to us, but now there is an alternative. For thousands of years, the Starship Earth has been sailing along without a captain, but the Captains can now appear—and it is all because of what takes place in the spiritual dimension. Physical weapons and physical means of protection cannot bring victory; Joshua taught us this lesson. As it is written, "Now Jericho was completely closed up because of the children of Israel: none went out, and none came in." There was, in other words, no chance of conquering Jericho; it was fortified like no other city before it. And what happened? The warriors surrounded the city: "So the people shouted, and [the priests] blew with the horns. And it came to pass, when the people heard the sound of the horn, that the people shouted with a great shout, and the wall fell down flat, so that the people went up into the city, with every man before him, and they took the city."

Joshua taught the people the correct meditation, which is also what we learn of *Rosh Hashanah*. That is the meaning of "the people shouted with a great shout." Here we see the tremendous power of mind and spirit directed against a fortification that could not be conquered by physical means.

Wars between nations and violent confrontations between individuals will come to an end only when we realize that such actions are a direct result of negative thought—and when we recognize that every physical manifestation of the thought must have an end. Jericho was physically impregnable, but it could not resist the thought consciousness of the *Shofar*. When negative energy meets positive energy, however, there is no doubt as to which will prevail. Positivity will always overcome negativity.

On an energetic level, the positive aspect appeared first and the negative aspect was but a result. This was the sequence of thought at the time of Creation. On the physical level, one can always move up the scale from rocks and spears to dynamite to the atom bomb. But how far does the scale reach? It ends when we face the kind of warfare that no longer takes place in the material dimension.

We are now engaged in nonphysical warfare. Yet at the same time, we have in our possession a method for positive energy transfer by means of which negative energies—those that create chaos of all kinds—will be subdued. Negative energy cannot resist the might of positive energy. And there is no need for us to try to improve the method we already have; there is no need to keep creating more so-called artillery, moving along the scale of destruction from Stone Age weapons to those of the nuclear era. That is because what we have is already perfect. Nothing can defeat the *Shofar*.

Of course, simply hearing the *Shofar* alone has no meaning and no power in itself; one must also "know" the *T'ruah*. It should be noted that the only word used in the Torah in this context is *T'ruah*. In the *Gemara*, however, the *Shevarim* and the *T'kiah* are mentioned as well. Why is this the case? It is because the Sages of the *Gemara* were not sure about the meaning of the word *T'ruah*. Is it a continuous sound emitted by the *Shofar*, or does it have breaks? And if so, how long are those breaks?

The *Shofar* was not used only on *Rosh Hashanah*. We have seen how, when they arrived in Israel and wished to conquer Jericho, the Israelites blew the *Shofar* and the walls came tumbling down. Similarly, *Yom Kippur* concludes with the blowing of the *Shofar*. And on *Yom Kippur* we speak of a *T'kiah*—one continuous sound. Yet only on *Rosh Hashanah* do we encounter a discussion of the meaning of the *T'ruah*. Are the sounds really that different? And if they are, what do they express, and why is it so important that we understand their meaning? Where does the order of the *Teki'ot* come from? And where did it originate?

In fact, the origin of this concept lies in *The Zohar*. To be sure, there are discussions of the issue in the Talmud as well. But if there is ever more than one opinion or point of view, the teachings of Kabbalah always prevail. The Law of Kabbalah always holds precedence over standard rulings.

Why did the Sages decide so? Because the Kabbalah deals not only with the sound of the *Shofar*, but with consciousness as well. Rav Shimon says that during the blowing of the *Shofar*, both the blower and his audience should inject consciousness into the sound. Put simply, the sound is like a telephone: As on the telephone, one must talk in order to manifest the connection. In every specific sound, according to Rav Shimon, both the consciousness of that sound and its objective are to be injected.

Once again, the order of the sounds is extremely complex. We blow the *Shofar* before the *Amidah* prayer as well as both during and after that prayer, and in each set of sounds there are several parts and stages. Nevertheless, according to Rav Shimon, even if we produce the correct sound at the correct times, our objective will not be achieved if we remain unaware of the specific energy transmitted at that specific moment. It is like a missile with no warhead: We need the warhead in order to hit the negative energy. The negative energy is that which creates the problems in our lives—and once we have removed it, everything will fall into place; every decision we make will be the right one.

There is a positive aspect and a negative aspect in each day of the year, and through the Ana Becho'ach prayer we are able to connect to the positive aspect. On *Rosh Hashanah*, however, a different system is in operation, and we cannot simply meditate in order to connect with the positive forces. The sole objective of the blowing of the *Shofar* is to destroy the negativity, which is expressed by pain, suffering, separation, sickness, and all other maladies included in the word *Din* (judgment). Thus, the coming year will be filled with happiness and certainty. Indeed, certainty is the Messiah. When there is certainty, there is everything. If everyone lived in certainty, then all decisions would be correct.

Decisions that have been injected with uncertainty really depend on nothing but luck, which is something on which we never wish to rely. But when uncertainty ceases to exists, we no longer need to know what the future will bring; we need only act in accordance with the teachings of Kabbalah, and the future will take care of itself. I do not have to take precautions in order to be protected from an uncertain future, because the way I act automatically leads me to the desired target.

According to Rav Shimon, there is only one way to move beyond uncertainty. Rav Shimon says that the word *T'ruah*, which is mentioned in the Torah, also includes the *Shevarim* and the *T'kiah*. But why is only the *T'ruah* mentioned? Rav Shimon says that there are two aspects to negativity—two *Gvurot*, meaning power, might, strength. These two energies are the left column (which is Isaac) and *Malchut* (which is David). Both energies symbolize negativity, but not in the evil sense of the word; rather, in the sense of the "minus" side. In an ordinary lightbulb, the negative pole is essential because it draws energy and brings about its manifestation. Similarly, it is the woman who becomes pregnant, since the "minus" side (the negative polarity in the case of the lightbulb) is that which manifests the energy. According to Rav Shimon, *Shevarim*, which is Isaac, and *T'ruah*, which is David, are the only two negative energies that exist in our world.

This shows us that negativity has two sides. But is a woman unable to give simply because she is negative? Certainly not. She has the power both to receive and to give. When we speak of Isaac, we refer to masculine power, and when we speak of *Malchut* we refer to feminine power. These two negative energies, and not the *Teki'ot*, are the spearheads. It is these energies that will destroy the judgments—the masculine and the feminine energies.

But what is the difference between these energies? The masculine energy has the quality of being dispatched outward, whereas the feminine energy remains within. For example, a table realizes itself in a certain location and does not affect its surroundings. If we wish to use it, we must approach it. A woman giving birth exerts masculine power, since she is creating life outside herself.

The negative energies are further divided into two categories, the first of which is the desire to receive for the self alone. This is a kind of energy that remains within. But there is also a negative energy that is projected outward. For example, perhaps you might want to give to your child, but the reason you want to do so is for your own sake rather than for hers. As a result, you smother her with goodness. In this case, you are indeed sharing your energy, but you are potentially destroying the child in the process. Even if you are sharing something good, giving can have a bad aspect if an exaggerated discharge of energy is involved.

Occasionally my ego may tell me that if I give to someone, I will be able to control that person—and this becomes the solitary reason for giving. The person then becomes dependent on me. Isaac, by contrast, represents energy that is dispatched outward in a balanced and measured manner. True sharing must be similarly balanced.

We previously noted that the lengths of the *Shevarim* and the *T'ruah* must be equal. Nevertheless, the sound of *Shevarim* is composed of three and the *T'ruah* of nine. Three soundings of the *T'ruah* are equivalent to one sounding of the *Shevarim*. Why? Rav Shimon says that the *Shevarim* are on a higher level. This refers to Isaac, who is in the upper triangle of the Shield of David (*Zeir Anpin*). The three soundings of *Shevarim* are right, left, and central column. But since we are talking about Isaac, each part in itself is united. When we descend from Isaac to *Malchut*, however, we enter into a separation of time, space, and motion. That is why the *T'ruah* is divided into nine sounds. In the Torah, only the word *T'ruah* is written. How, then, did Rav Shimon and the Talmud develop the word *Shevarim*? The answer is that the *T'ruah* contains the *Shevarim* in a concealed fashion. The *T'ruah* is on a higher level of potential energy.

We have stated before that the *T'ruah* and the *Shevarim* are the energetic spearheads. But if this is the case, why do we need the preliminary *T'kiah* and the concluding *T'kiah*? The *Teki'ot* are not energies. The first *T'kiah* is Abraham; this is its code. We know from the Torah that Abraham came to bind (*le'ekod*), to connect. When we encounter a great flow of energy, a great flow of ideas, we cannot connect them unless they are activated. *Akeda*, or binding, means to connect everything together.

The first *T'kiah* efficiently and accurately activates the spearheads, *T'ruah* and *Shevarim*. It ensures that we take advantage of the energy we have in the missile in the most efficient and accurate way possible. This is the intention of the binding of Isaac, the binding of the negative energy.

The final *T'kiah* is Jacob, the central column. Here the objective is to stabilize the missile. As in a lightbulb, the positive and negative poles are not sufficient to create a circuit; resistance is also required. Therefore, on the last *T'kiah* we must push the activating button, which is Jacob.

This brings us to an understanding of the name *Tishrei*. It is clear to us that this is a code of the Torah. The Aramaic letter *Tav* is the *T'kiah*; the *Shin* stands for *Shevarim*, the *Resh* for *T'ruah*, and the *Yud* for the final *T'kiah*. It can thus be seen that *Tishrei* is not just a name; there is a coded message within it that is deciphered by Kabbalah.

Why do we execute the *T'ruah* and the *Shevarim*? Are they not inherently negative? Let us compare it to a vaccine that contains a virus. Isaac and David are not evil, but they embody a measure of negativity. Yet not all negative energy is evil; it depends on how that energy is put to use. Indeed, using negative energy is the only means by which we can subdue Satan. Therefore, only by including the negative channels of Isaac and David can the vaccine be created. We thus encircle Isaac and David with Abraham (the desire to give) and with Jacob (the force of resistance) and in this way create a vaccine—a spiritual missile, an invincible sound of the *Shofar*.

Using the cycle of prayers and the knowledge we have just acquired, we can destroy—or at least diminish—the power of Satan that exists throughout the universe. As we know, in kabbalistic meditation we are dealing with two aspects. The first is the personal aspect, which concerns only the individual, and the second is the collective aspect, which deals with the fragmentation that exists in the universe. Even if only two people—or two million people—succeed in decreasing the power of Satan, the universe as a whole will benefit from their actions. When mankind is in a state of "love your neighbor as yourself," all human suffering will vanish.

What often prevents people of all faiths from connecting to the desire to share is the fact that the universe is so heavily laden with negative energy. The intensity of this energy is so strong that even good people fall into the trap. Yet we can create the new year as no year has been created before. The greater the number of people who are engaged in true reality without physical illusion, and the greater the number who broaden their awareness rather than falling into deep sleep, the sooner we will witness the arrival of the Messiah, which signals the transformation of all mankind.

In section nine of *Gate of Meditations*, The Ari discusses the *Shofar* and the *Teki'ot* at great length. A number of explanations are presented by The Ari, but Rav Chaim Vital, who transcribed The Ari's teachings, chooses what he believes will best clarify the issue. For example: How is the word *Shofar* composed? שׁוֹ (*Shin Vav*) is 306 in numerology. Together with the 14 finger joints, which hold the *Shofar*, we obtain 320 (it is known that the reason the hand is called יָד (*yad*) is because it has 14 finger joints: three in each finger and two in the thumb, totaling 14). It can then be seen that 306 +14 = 320, which are the 320 sparks "*Shin Vav + Yud Dalet*"—that is, the original Light that was revealed during the Big Bang. We encounter this phenomenon when the Light comes toward us and we reflect it. The concept of reflection is similar to that of an iron rod hitting a boulder and producing sparks. Thus were the 320 sparks—the origin of all souls in the world—created.

What is the meaning of the word *Shofar*? The Aramaic names of all physical entities in the world indicate their inner meaning. The first part, the שׁוֹ (*Shin Vav*), together with the 14 finger joints, are the 320 sparks that connect us to the interior of all sparks of Light in the world.

The last two letters are פ (*Peh*), ר (*Resh*). What is special about the animal named *parah*, or bull? The Ari writes that the meaning here lies in the "five *Gvurot* of the final letters"—the five "final letters" of the Aramaic alphabet ך ף ץ ן ם (*Mem*

Nun Tzadi Pei Caf). The letters themselves are an illusion, but it is important for us to know what metaphysical consciousness is included in them. These five levels of *Gvurot*—that is to say, the five degrees of eternal energy of judgments—are aroused and revealed through them.

Gvurah acts like the negative pole in a lightbulb. Without it, the flow within the electrical wire exists in only a potential state, and no use can be made of it. *Gvurah* closes the circuit and activates that light. It is much the same with the five "final letters." Before the Sin of the Golden Calf, the Israelites had access to these letters and knew how to use them in order to manifest the totality of all the Light that could come into the world. After the Sin of the Golden Calf, however, that knowledge was taken away from them.

Today, how can the totality of the power of Light be manifested? It can be accomplished through the use of these five letters. Then, when all the Light in the world is revealed, everything becomes a living entity and is no longer a still object. Thus, with the aid of the *mantzepach* ךֿ םֿ ץֿ ןֿ ףֿ, we can achieve resurrection of the dead and activate a force of continuity in all areas of life.

The five final letters are the five *Gvurot* that come from *Binah.* *Binah* is the energy storehouse from which flows all the Light that may be revealed in our world, and the five final letters are the same numerology as *Pei Resh* (= 280), which is the communication channel that allows for the execution of the Light of *Binah* in the world of *Malchut.* Par, the bull, coupled with the five fingers holding the *Shofar*, is also related to the issue of the Red Heifer.

The five fingers represent the completion of the Tree of Life, and therefore they are the perfect conduits for the desire to receive. If we had no fingers, we would not be able to achieve our wish. The five fingers are the medium by which we may grasp the entire world.

Thus, the Aramaic word *Shofar* contains both the 320 sparks of energy that are in the universe and the bull. Two letters represent the sparks themselves, and two represent the actual system of *Gvurot*, through which everything merges into the single concept called the *Shofar*. The *Shofar* is therefore transformed from a simple object, a ram's horn, into a communications apparatus for all sparks of life in the universe, as well as a system of five *Gvurot* that realizes these sparks in the physical world.

This is why we use the *Shofar*. As The Ari explains, it is in this way that we rid ourselves of all the negativity in our lives. It would be foolish indeed to imagine that simply saying "I'm sorry" could ever be sufficient to this task, for doing so does not eliminate any negative energy. To the contrary, the only way to discard negativity is to remove it from the entire universe—for if darkness remains anywhere, the entire world will be affected by it. As The Ari explains, since *Binah* is the energy storehouse of the totality of the Light, we require the same connection with *Binah* in order to rid the world of darkness.

On page 257 of *Gate of Meditations*, The Ari specifically demystifies the blowing of the *Shofar* by describing how to blow the *Shofar*, in what sequence to do so, and with what meditations. In it he also explains how to use the *Shofar* to achieve the objectives we have defined for ourselves.

Tav Shin Resh Tav, Tav Shin Tav, Tav Resh Tav are the acronyms of the various blowings. In the first section we blow *T'kiah-Shevarim-T'ruah-T'kiah*; in the second, *T'kiah-Shevarim-T'kiah*; and finally, in the third, *T'kiah-T'ruah-T'kiah*. A *T'kiah* is always sounded at the beginning and at the end of each combination. This encircles the judgments between the right and central columns, thereby reducing and balancing them.

This entire procedure, which is called three times *meyushhav*, is repeated three times. The first sequence of blowings is called meyushav, or settled, while the subsequent blowings are performed during the *Amidah* prayer. We blow the series *Tav Shin Resh Tav, Tav Shin Tav, Tav Resh Tav* three times during the silent *Amidah* prayer, and then again during the repetition by the prayer leader. The meyushav has 30 sounds, the silent *Amidah* another 30 sounds, and the repetition of the *Amidah* 40 sounds—for a total of 100 sounds. Why 100? Because 100 is the totality of the Tree of Life (10 times the 10 Sfirot), totaling 100 packets of energy.

Communication takes place through our knowledge and implementation of the meditations, for actions performed on the physical level radiate to the spiritual level—to *Zeir Anpin* and to *Binah*. Only when we are aware of what we are doing and use the *Shofar* in an informed manner can we reduce and balance the *Din* and connect with the totality of the *Shofar*.

The Ari writes that the Aramaic letters הוהי (*Yud Hei Vav Hei*) are the Tetragrammaton. They are its potential state. Spelling out the names of these letters manifests the Holy name and connects it with our world. Through the *Shofar*, we intend to connect to *Binah* so that we may return all the energy executed in the form of judgments to the energy storehouse—for it is only in this way that we will remove the destructive energy from ourselves and from the universe.

The Zohar says that a set of 100 sounds must be sounded from the *Shofar*, and The Ari explains why: Before being pronounced, the letters *Yud Hei Vav Hei* are the potential. Their utterance realizes them. It is as if we were clothing the letters, and in doing so restricting them. After accessing the letters in their fully spelled form, they may be pronounced, for they are no longer in a potential state. The pronunciation of the fully spelled letters then realizes their hidden potential. *Binah* is connected to the Tetragrammaton. The letters are ו (*Vav*) *Dalet*, which complete the *Yud*; *Yud*, which completes the *Hei*; Aleph *Vav*, which complete the *Vav*; and *Yud*, which completes the final *Hei*. The numerical values of all the letters used to fully spell the letters is 37, which is also the value of הבל (*hevel*), or breath —the same breath required for the blowing of the *Shofar*. The blowing is the clothing and the spelling-out, as are the pronunciation of the letters and the words. סג (*Samech gimel*) is 63, and it is the spiritual, potential description of the connection to *Binah*. Adding the letters amounts to 37 + 63 = 100. Therefore, through the system of letters insinuated in the blowings of the *Shofar*, we are able to be elevated to *Binah*.

The *Shofar* is transformed into a physical expression of
the large spiritual *Shofar—Binah*, which includes all the sparks
as well as the five *Gvurot* that execute them. The word
לְמַעְלָה (*lema'ala*), or above, does not mean "high in the
sky"; rather, עֶלְיוֹן (*elyon*), or upper, is something that has
not been given material expression. The moment something is
given material expression, it becomes restricted and minimized.

When we focus on something, we restrict it—just as we
do when we zoom in with a camera. We restrict the field of
vision, and in return we see the focused area more clearly. In
order to see a single detail more clearly, in other words, we forfeit the other parts of the picture. The same principle also links
the spiritual potential and the realization of everything in the
world. If a cup were connected to totality, for example, it would
not be possible for us to fill that cup with water, because in its
infinite and complete state, it would be totally spiritual. In order
to create a cup, we must therefore take the atoms from the
source of their being, shape them in a manner that creates a material cup, and in the process reduce the atoms to a limited state.

The blowing of the *Shofar* is often described as a "tradition"—a means of catching the Creator's attention and causing
Him to look upon us with mercy. For all those who believe this,
the *Shofar* will indeed remain no more than a simple, small
object. And for them, the sounding of the *Shofar* will continue
to be no more than an act that is repeated at a certain time of
the year, and the objectives of which The Ari spoke will remain
far beyond their grasp.

The *Shofar* is constructed with a small opening at one end and a wider opening at the other, from which sound is emitted. The more consciousness we introduce, the more we accomplish on the *Shofar*, as the object itself is just the physical horn of a ram. Kabbalistically, of course, we are dealing not only with a ram's horn but also with its metaphysical reality. In this way, we increase its significance and value, and draw closer to the great *Shofar* that is concealed within.

Why did the Creator create the ram's horn with a narrow opening close to the blower's mouth and a wide-outlet opening? The answer is concealed in the verse "Out of dire straits I called upon Hashem." Before the blowing of the *Shofar*, we say this verse as well as other verses, such as קְרַע שָׂטָן (*Krah Satan*) (the second verse of the Ana Becho'ach), which is interpreted as "I have called God from a state in which I am living in oppression and need." It is known that the Creator has many names, and *Yud Hei* is one of them. This verse appears to be a cry for help that is directed by the worshipper toward the Creator of the world. But The Ari reveals that the subject here is not really prayer, but rather a description of the structure of the *Shofar*.

The concept of *Rosh Hashanah* is mentioned in the portion of *Pinchas*, Section 29, verse 1, which reads, "And in the seventh month, on the first day of the month, you shall have a holy convocation: you shall do no manner of servitude; it is a day of blowing the horn unto you."

We know that *T'ruah* is one of the sounds produced by the *Shofar* on *Rosh Hashanah*. The others, *T'kiah* and *Shevarim*, are not mentioned explicitly in the Torah. Nor, for that matter, does the Torah describe the way in which the *T'kiah*, the *T'ruah*, and the *Shevarim* are to be performed. The passage above is the only verse that appears in the Torah regarding the *Shofar* blowings. Why is only one verse written about such an important holiday? New Moons, for example—which are far less important than *Rosh Hashanah*—are mentioned many more times. In like manner, the Torah deals in great detail with the holidays of *Pesach* and *Shavuot*, but when it comes to *Rosh Hashanah*, it is brief. Why?

Rav Shimon took the man who was to be the prayer leader and purified him for three days. The person blowing the *Shofar* must be at an even higher level of purity than that required of a prayer leader. In order for the missiles to hit their targets, perfect as those missiles might be, the launch pad must be in perfect working order as well. Therefore, Rav Shimon emphasizes the importance of the prayer leader, who acts, in effect, as a launch pad.

All the negativity injected by people into the universe will one day come to haunt each and every one of them. From Rav Shimon, we understand that on *Rosh Hashanah* two things are called for: First, we must understand what is taking place; and second, the prayer leader or the person blowing the *Shofar* should be qualified for his job, because he himself is the system.

Why did Rav Shimon invest so much time in training the prayer leader and the *Shofar* blower? It is because he encountered the same problems that we confront today. Most people who are not yet involved in the study of Kabbalah regard *Rosh Hashanah* as a holiday that unifies everyone—not unlike the *Pesach Seder*, which appears to unify the family. But the fact that an entire family is gathered together does not necessarily mean that it is unified. In order for a family to be unified, it might indeed be necessary for them to sit together, but this alone will not fulfill the objective. Instead, it is only through the performance of the *Seder*—which is a method that includes prayers and other activities—that the unity of the family will be ensured. For *Rosh Hashanah*, however, the requirement of being together is not mentioned in the Torah. According to Rav Shimon, the single verse in the Torah that deals with *Rosh Hashanah* indicates that this day is a day of *T'ruah*, meaning distress or lamentation.

When does one lament? On sorrowful occasions, at distressful events. This, then, is what *Rosh Hashanah* is concerned with. It is a day that contains a single idea, the concept of the *T'ruah*. Things fall apart on this day; the world stands to be judged. In contradistinction to *Pesach*, gathering the family together on *Rosh Hashanah* will not patch up the pieces. Instead, it remains a fragmented day. On this day, there is not enough energy in the universe to allow sitting together to result in any change. If we do not attack the negative consciousness of *Din* on this day, it will persecute us throughout the year. And this is what Rav Shimon is emphasizing: The fact that we physically sit together and attempt to be united in a physical way will not suffice to remove the traces of our past negative actions on *Rosh Hashanah*, because this activity cannot be removed by any means other than prayer and the *Shofar*.

Of course, it is not enough just to hear the blowing of the *Shofar*. In addition, we must consciously focus on the internal energy of each sounding. This matter is discussed in the biblical commentaries known as the *Gemara*, in which the Sages all come to the conclusion that fulfilling precepts requires intention and awareness. Without this, the objective cannot be achieved. By way of illustration, the *Gemara* proposes the example of a person who does not wish to hear the *Shofar*, but who happens to pass near a synagogue at the moment in which it sounds. A related example concerns a man who is forced to eat *matzah* on *Pesach*. Do these people gain the benefits of the *Shofar* and the *matzah?* The answer is no.

More than other holidays, *Pesach* is connected to the material world, and the *Seder* is an expression of that bond. On *Rosh Hashanah*, however, nothing is connected to the physical realm. To make this clear, the *Gemara* reminds us that we do not bless the new moon on the Shabbat before *Rosh Hashanah*. *Tishrei* is the only month in which the new moon is not blessed on the preceding Shabbat.

There are many explanations for this, but one of the most common explanations reminds us that since there is an aspect of judgment involved in *Rosh Hashanah*, we do not want to remind God or Satan of the arrival of the Day of Judgment. For this reason, it is said, we do not mention it on the Shabbat before *Rosh Hashanah*.

To be sure, this is the explanation that is most frequently given. Rashi, however, offers a different one: "The moon is not apparent." But was Rashi mistaken here? Step outdoors at this time of year and you'll see the moon quite clearly. So what did Rashi mean? He quotes from the Book of Psalms: "Blow the horn at the new moon, at the full moon for our feast day" (Tehilim 81:4). On this day the moon is concealed. But if this is so, what is the moonlike object we see in the sky? It is an illusion! This can be compared to a decapitated chicken that continues to run around even without a head. The chicken is not alive just because we see it moving. Similarly, the power of illusion is strong on *Rosh Hashanah* because it is the day on which judgment rules. Negativity is in control, and separation reigns. No day is as negative as *Rosh Hashanah*.

Even on the ninth of *Av*, the day on which the Satan rules, there is a defense system. After all, this is the day on which the Messiah is born. The ninth of *Av* has a protective shield, so all we have to do is connect to it. On *Rosh Hashanah* there is no such protective shield, and there is nothing on which we can rely. On this day, even the Creator sits on the Throne of Judgment rather than on the Throne of Mercy. The ninth of *Av* has a positive aspect. On *Rosh Hashanah*, there is not even a bit of positivity.

A Deeper Look at
Rosh Hashanah

Rosh Hashanah is described in the Torah as the "Feast of the *Shofar*," the holiday celebrated on the first and second days of the month of *Tishrei*. In Numbers 29:1, it is written, "And in the seventh month, on the first day of the month, you shall have a holy convocation: you shall do no manner of servitude; it is a day of blowing the horn unto you."

According to Yechezkel 30:1, the name *"Rosh Hashanah"* refers to the beginning of the year. In Exodus 12:2, it is written, "This month (*Nissan*) shall be unto you the beginning of months; it shall be the first month of the year to you." At first glance, this would appear to be a contradiction: Is *Tishrei* the first month of the year, or is it *Nissan*, the month of Exodus from Egypt? And what is the meaning of the name *Tishrei*? Moreover, why the *Shofar*? Why blow it? And yet another question: Holidays such as *Pesach*, *Shavuot*, and *Sukkot* are celebrated in the Diaspora for two days. In Israel, however, it was possible to celebrate for only one day, since the exact time of the birth of the moon was known. Why, then, is *Rosh Hashanah* celebrated in Israel for two days? Why is one day not sufficient?

The sign of *Tishrei* is Libra, and the word Libra in Aramaic, *moznaim* (scales), can help us answer these questions. Put simply, the month of *Tishrei* is a month of trial.

The kabbalists understood that since the month in question is the seventh month, we are dealing with the number seven. Here our knowledge is enhanced by the language of numerology, without which there could be no physics, no science, and no Kabbalah. The seventh month is *Malchut*, the dimension of the desire to receive—and there is no force in the entire universe like the human being's desire to receive.

The significance of *Rosh Hashanah* lies in the cosmic balance of the sign of Libra. According to Kabbalah, a person's vessel for receiving energy in the coming year is based on his activity during the year that has just ended. Furthermore, the activity of each individual influences the distribution of energy in the universal reservoir. Will there be energy for everyone, or will there be some who, heaven forbid, receive no energy at all?

According to *the Book of Formation*, the month of *Tishrei* is controlled by the planet Venus. This combination of Venus and Libra creates in *Tishrei* the Day of Judgment—the cosmic event that enables us to remove Bread of Shame. But can we be granted life each year without accepting responsibility, without committing to the removal of Bread of Shame? Our "package," after all, includes one day in court with Satan, and with the evidence that he has gathered against us in the course of the previous year. The Creator, acting as judge, does not mix in considerations of mercy on this day, although mercy is indeed one of His attributes.

The Day of Judgment is a cosmic event that is determined at the time of Creation. At this time, each soul is examined in order to determine whether it and the body in which it dwells have the potential to remove Bread of Shame or, conversely, whether an additional year will bring nothing more than futility—a continuation of the desire to receive for the self alone. Why go on if change is not possible?

Time is relative, and time differs from person to person. What is truly important is how our time is filled. It is said that there are those who live 70 years as if it were one day, and those who in one day live 70 years. If year after year we do not remove Bread of Shame, what basis do we have for requesting energy for an additional year? In such a case, the soul has not succeeded in its present incarnation—so perhaps the time has come for it to move into another body. The soul may wish to perform the task, but what is the point of living in this condition for another year?

The Day of Judgment is about reflecting on our own actions—and according to the Talmud, three books are opened on this day: the Book of Life, the Book of Death, and another book concerning those who are in between and must be given another chance. To grasp the meaning of this, we must first understand the connection to the age in which we live, the Age of Aquarius. For 2,000 years, people have been visiting synagogues, specifically on *Rosh Hashanah*, knowing practically nothing about the holiday itself. This may have been acceptable for centuries, but new questions are now being posed. The traditional framework that once sufficed for the existence of a religion no longer holds today.

Once a year, the cosmic auditor arrives in order to record each individual's profit-and-loss statement. The objective of this calculation is to examine whether the continuation of each person's life will benefit his soul in light of his actions during the previous year. This is not unlike a debate that is waged to determine the fate of a company, with the outcome hinging on that company's balance sheet and profit-and-loss statement. This, then, is what *Rosh Hashanah* is all about: It is the day on which a determination is made as to whether an existing body should continue or whether the soul requires a change of shape. And the verdict ultimately rests on one's past performance, which attests to the chance that the correction, or *tikkun*, will be performed. If there is such a chance, the body is given additional energy and is granted the capacity to continue for another year. All this takes place on the Day of Judgment. It can thus be seen that someone who enters a synagogue on this day and prays without knowing why, can be likened to a company that is given a loan from a bank but immediately squanders it. There is no purpose in such a loan, as the balance sheet will show that the additional funds did not reap any benefit at all. And if the scales show an insolvent business, why carry on? So why pray? Why blow the *Shofar*?

The cosmic code provides us with a full understanding of what takes place during the first days of the month of *Tishrei*. This, the seventh month, is related to *Malchut*, the desire to receive. In the seventh month, the desire to receive is, as it were, cross-examined on the witness stand with regard to its actions during the past year. Because the desire to receive is on trial, and because human life is in fact an expression of the desire to receive, each person is judged in this manner in the seventh month.

During this trial, each person sees a playback of all his actions within the past year. The prosecutor then tries to establish that the entity in question is failing. We, for our part, hope for another chance, even if the scale shows that there is little evidence to justify our hope. Then, on the first day of *Tishrei*, Satan—the prosecutor—demands a sentence of death. So when the scales of justice indicate that we have failed, what are we to do? The answer is this: We can blow the *Shofar*. But as we have said before, merely blowing the *Shofar* will not suffice. If we do not know the power of the *Shofar* and do not have the clear intention of bringing that power into our lives, no connection will be made.

But why is the trial held on the first day of the sign of Libra? *The Zohar* reveals that the sun and moon were both created on the fourth day, but that the moon was told to remain concealed. On this day the moon—*Malchut*, the desire to receive—was without Light. Therefore, the first man was born with a desire to receive that was concealed from Light. And this is why judgment has a chance to express itself in court on this day. The origin of the word mozna'im—meaning balance, or scales (also Libra)—is *ozen*, or ear. But what do scales have to do with the ear? The ear has three tiny bones that make hearing possible. And the reason it has three parts derives from its relationship to *Binah*. *Binah* is the next step in human evolution and is a three-part combination of "right," "left," and "central."

Binah represents the energy storehouse from which all forms of cosmic energy derive. And when *the Book of Formation* refers to the month of *Tishrei* as the month of Libra (scales), it gives us a clue as to what we can do on the Day of Judgment when our balance sheet is negative. *The Book of Formation* also notes that the Aramaic letter ל (*Lamed*) created *Tishrei* and Libra, and it is no coincidence that the letter is composed of three components: upper, middle, and lower. This reveals the "secret of three," representing the three books that are opened on *Rosh Hashanah*: the Book of Life, which is right column; the Book of Death, which is left column; and the middle book, which is central column. According to *The Zohar*, what we aim to do on *Rosh Hashanah* is nothing less than to attack Satan, which is the essence of our negative activity, and one that can bring death upon us. As *The Zohar* clearly specifies, if we succeed in fooling Satan on *Rosh Hashanah* while he pleads his case against us—if we can prevent him from presenting our negative information—we can automatically receive an injection of energy from *Binah*.

Let us now examine an additional clue presented to us by the Torah. We call the holiday "*Rosh Hashanah*." Yet the word *rosh* (head) expresses more than just the concept of a beginning.

Rosh, in the kabbalistic sense, means the maximum infusion of energy, the spearhead. Therefore, all energy required by all human beings for the entire year can be found on this day. We must all find this energy, and we must then direct it so that it will enable us to live our everyday lives in peace and tranquillity.

Binah is the reservoir of energy and understanding from which the world began. As it is written in the first verse of Genesis, "In the beginning God created the heaven and the earth." But was the heaven not created on the fourth day? What is the heaven if not the universe and the heavenly bodies within it? How is it that the first verse already deals with the heaven and the earth? And as to the earth, it is written in Genesis 1:9, which describes the third day of Creation, "And God said: "Let the waters under the heaven be gathered together unto one place, and let the dry land appear."

To understand this, we must first remember that the Torah is a code. Let us thus consider the following: "In the beginning (*Beresheet*), [God] created (*barah*)." The word *Beresheet* contains the word *rosh* (head) because this is the beginning. But where was the beginning? The word *barah* is in fact a code for the energy that is stored in *Binah*. But what is *Binah*, and why is it important that we understand its significance in relation to our lives?

Throughout the entire process of Creation, there are two aspects: heaven and earth. These aspects do not, however, refer to the physical heaven and earth. It is critical that we understand this distinction, because it is one that goes to the heart of the split between science and religion—a false dichotomy that has persisted for far too long. In point of fact, there is no real contradiction between the Torah and science.

But how can this be the case, since it is written that the world was created in six days, and yet the world has been in existence for 5765 years? Does this not contradict scientific findings? The answer is no. When we discuss the days of Creation, we are not referring to time in a linear sense. It must be understood that the heaven and earth referred to here are *Zeir Anpin* and *Malchut*, the sun and the moon—the energy of the desire to share and that of the desire to receive. These energies were created at the outset with the configuration of thought consciousness, without material realization—and that is what Creation refers to. The seven days thus have no relation at all to "days" in the conventional sense of the word.

Genesis 1:27 deals with the creation of male and female. Here it is written, "And God created man in His own image, in the image of God created He him; male and female created He them." We know, however, that in Genesis 2 the story of the Creation of Man is told, and in verse 7 it is written, "Hashem formed man of the dust of the ground, and breathed into his nostrils the breath of life; and man became a living soul." Later, in verse 18, we read, "And Hashem, God said: 'It is not good that the man should be alone; I will make him a help meet for him.' " From Adam's rib, Eve was created in verse 21. But didn't this already take place in Genesis 1? According to Kabbalah, Chapter 1 of the Book of Genesis refers to the pure thought—the Creation with the configuration of thought consciousness.

But what does the "creation of thought" really mean? The answer is that it is similar to the Creation of Man. Before everything we do, a thought exists, and that thought must be created prior to its realization. Genesis 1 speaks only of the pure energy of thought. But on the fourth day, there is a separation between *Zeir Anpin* and *Malchut*, between the energy of thought of the desire to give and that of the desire to receive. And it is there that the separation originates. This is man—and it is man who has forgotten his objective, the essence of which is how to receive. But without the positive and negative poles, the electrical circuit cannot exist. So this is what was created on the first day: the positive and the negative. And they were equal; there was the desire to receive (negative) just as there was the desire to share (positive). But the fourth day, on which *Malchut* separated from the desire to share, is the first day of *Rosh Hashanah*. And it is there that the negative thought consciousness of the desire to receive for the self alone was born.

Therefore Satan—the pure negative energy of the desire to receive for the self alone—was born on this day as well. Yet the creation of Satan and of this negative energy was necessary, for had we been completely balanced—had there been a balance between the desire to share and the desire to receive—how would we then remove Bread of Shame? The reason for our existence must not be forgotten, and that reason lies in nothing more than the removal of Bread of Shame. Our sole objective in life is to create inner balance. And only when this inner balance exists is it possible for us to tap into the energy storehouse of *Binah*, which nurtures both *Zeir Anpin* and *Malchut*. If, however, our past performance points to a negative balance—that is, if we have allowed the last 365 days to be fragmented, to be disconnected from the desire to share—then Satan will appear. It can thus be seen that on *Rosh Hashanah*—on the fourth day of Creation—the separation between the desire to receive and the desire to share was created, and it was then that Satan appeared and began to persecute us.

Upon coming to *Binah*—the realm of the Creation, the energy storeroom—we submit a petition, a request, for an energy budget for the coming year. But can we, who have created chaos within the cosmic structure, demand of the universe energetic support for our actions? And if so, what are we to do with the evidence that has been gathered against us? How is it conceivable that without a physical connection, we may enter into the supersensory domain of the universe and tip the negative scale that bars our access to the energy storehouse? This is difficult to understand.

Kabbalah deals with technologies for controlling the spiritual dimension of the universe—a dimension that is perceived only by the soul. Our physical bodies have no idea as to the nature of these forces. The power of a nuclear bomb cannot be likened to the great power of the universe, a force more powerful than that of the sun. But can we control such a force? The answer is yes—for the entire objective of Creation is to empower man to control all so that he may remove Bread of Shame. If there were something man could not control, how could he control his fate? Man could have come to the Creator and said to him: You have created the universe in such a way that I don't stand a chance. You have created me as a Scorpio or as a Leo, and I have no way to counter the cosmic influences that affect this sign. So must I be responsible for my actions?

The answer to this question is yes, we must take that responsibility—because everything that exists is created in such a way that man may have free choice with respect to the fate of the universe. If the universe is in chaos, then it is a result of human activity alone. Man is in full control of the universe, consciously or not. Even when we are acting according to the desire to receive for the self alone, says The Ari, we create negative energetic entities that eventually return to create our physical and spiritual DNA. Therefore, when a saddening event occurs, we have no one to blame but ourselves. To be sure, this approach runs counter to most other schools of thought, religious or otherwise. But until we understand the true nature of reality, we will never achieve real security, either collectively as a species or as individual human beings.

Rosh Hashanah is a day that encompasses a complete cycle of 365 days, because each year it re-creates the condition of Genesis 1, when we brought into being the desire to receive for the self alone. We must also ask, however, why there is a 365-day cycle at all. The Torah responds that there are 365 negative forces in the universe, each of which is expressed by one of the 365 restrictions of the Torah. Each one of these restrictions— "thou shalt not steal," for example—is a code representing the negative forces. And each day of the year has its own negative force that is connected to the desire to receive for the self alone. In point of fact, if we closely examine the days on which certain crimes were committed throughout history, we will indeed begin to discern a pattern. We will also discover a pattern with respect to the times of day in which certain negative events take place. For example, it has been found that most crimes take place between 5 p.m. and 7 p.m. These are the hours before sunset, and Kabbalah teaches that the sun sets not because of its astronomical position but because of the negative energy that is present after noon, which reaches its peak at the time of sunset. There is, in other words, a spiritual force at work.

Most people feel at their best in the morning. Why? Is it because the sun is shining? But why does it shine? The kabbalists explain that the morning is suffused by the positive cosmic energy called *Chesed*, the desire to share, and that sharing reveals energy. The negative desire to receive for the self limits the energy storehouse from giving out the energy it would have liked to give. The Creator has no intention of creating sorrow and suffering for mankind, but on each day there is a different negative force that was created so that we may remove Bread of Shame. If not a day went by when I had the desire to steal, then I would have remained a "good boy" only because nothing had motivated me in the other direction. There are forces in the universe that cause certain people, and not others, to steal. Therefore, at the end of the 365-day cycle, we return to *Rosh Hashanah*—the Day of Judgment, the Day of Darkness, the day on which one may not beg for mercy. The only thing taken into account on this day is the balance of our actions.

We have asked why *Rosh Hashanah* has two days. The Talmud answers: *Yomah arichtah* (Aramaic for "it is a long day"). In point of fact, all of *Rosh Hashanah* is one long day. So are there 24 hours in a day, or 48? And why is there suddenly one 48-hour day? We have seen that each day of the year has been given a certain negative energy. According to The Ari, these negative energies are divided into two categories, one of which is called harsh judgment. This is the hard core of the desire to receive for the self alone, which encompasses hatred, murder, and other terrible restrictions. If on the first day we do not destroy, by means of the *Shofar*, the negative energy of the desire to receive for the self alone, then the energy storehouse referred to by the code name *Binah* will remain closed.

The second day of *Rosh Hashanah* represents a different aspect of the Day of Judgment. This second day is concerned with "softer" judgments. Anyone who does not get through the first day—for example, someone who had hatred for no reason—has his fate determined on this day. But if in the Book of Life it is said that we have made an effort to live according to the tenet "love your neighbor as yourself," we will not have to wage the harshest battle. Yet there is still a battle to be waged. If a person does not tend to the pain of others whom they could have helped, or if someone accedes to any other desire to receive for the self alone, he must be aware of what awaits him. When that person approaches the energy storeroom and requests energy for a whole year, the Storekeeper is bound to debit his account for the smaller tasks he has not completed. This takes place on the second day, which deals with misdeeds that were less negative than those judged on the day before. In any case, we must pay for such misdeeds. They have been debited, and we must ask for credit.

Our overall task on *Rosh Hashanah* is to ensure that the coming year will be filled with positive energy, with no chaos of any kind. This holiday is about giving all human beings an opportunity to shape their lives for the next 365 days. And for that purpose, two days of battle are needed. In the Land of Israel, many holidays—including *Sukkot*, *Pesach*, and *Shavuot*—are celebrated for one day only. This stands in contrast to the Diaspora, where all holidays are celebrated for two days. *Rosh Hashanah* is an exception because it is celebrated for two days even in Israel.

Just as we have a soul and a body—just as a cup has an interior and an exterior, just as everything has a physical aspect that is evident and a spiritual aspect that is concealed—so does *Rosh Hashanah* have two days.

In the days of The Temple, *Rosh Hashanah* was celebrated for one day only, because at that time prayers had the power to elevate the physical body of the worshipper to a higher level of consciousness, to the World of Formation. In the days of The Temple, when the Israelites dwelled in the Land of Israel, they attracted and transmitted spiritual abundance not only to all nations of the world, but to the entire universe. Peace and harmony are a necessary result of the ascent to the 99% spiritual reality.

But why is this the case? Consider the crime of theft. Why steal if theft can bring profit only within the limited 1% world? One cannot steal happiness, health, or love. To the contrary, our Sages succeeded in bringing these things into their lives only through the application of the kabbalistic knowledge embodied in the Torah. We are following in their footsteps with a similar intent and goal.

Today, however, since prayer alone cannot elevate physical consciousness to the World of Formation, we have additional methods that can assist us in this process.

The Aramaic word *Tefilah* (prayer) comes from the word *Tafel* (bland). The practical activity of fulfilling a Mitzvah is connected to the World of Action. Therefore, its effect on the physical body is greater. With regard to this, *The Zohar* describes a meeting that took place between the Yanukah, the six-year-old son of Rav Hamenuna Saba (also called the Great Fish), and several students of Rav Shimon. On this day the Yanukah, who through use of Divine Inspiration could see beyond time and space, did not greet these students because he knew that they had not recited the Shma reading that day. In response, the students said that they had been busy from early morning collecting contributions for a wedding and assisting in burying a deceased—and it is known that "he who performs a Mitzvah is exempt from a Mitzvah." The practical occupation with Mitzvot had, in other words, exempted the students from prayer on that day. Their spiritual work had achieved what the prayer had been intended to achieve, and more.

On the first day of *Rosh Hashanah*, the internal aspect of the soul ascends, and the external aspect ascends on the second—that is to say, our consciousness ascends first, and our physical manifestation follows. It is like throwing a stone into water: Even though the stone has already been thrown, waves will not appear until the stone hits the surface of the water. In order to receive the full effect of *Rosh Hashanah*, spiritual ascent must be performed in both consciousness and body.

But why is the first day one of harsh judgment—one that is related to serious transgressions and disorder in life? The reason is this: Since there is no actual revelation of Light (the Light is in only a potential state), there can be no influence on the physical world. Therefore, the law of restriction is in force, and this law states that the potential will remain concealed. The moment the stone left the hand in its flight toward the water, the concentric circles had already begun to form, but only in potential—just as a seed potentially contains a tree and its fruit. Both the tree and the fruit already exist in the 99% realm, but they are not yet present in the physical realm, and therefore they are not yet visible.

The eye is indeed restricted in that it can see things only after they materialize. Moreover, when two persons witness a certain event, each of them will testify to having witnessed an entirely different scene. This is because the 1% realm never loses its property of restriction. Our consciousness, however, already perceives the events in their potential state. In effect, the mind "sees" the event before it occurs, and the event itself is actually a reconstruction that takes place according to the impression of the mind rather than the sight of the eye.

Let us remember that within the 99% limited world, spiritual energy is unencumbered by restrictions of time, space, or motion. One person may view a particular channel of occurrence, while another may watch a different channel altogether. Since the eye cannot detect information that was not previously evident to the mind, each spectator sees the details of an event differently. In addition, the eye restricts the image that the mind sees. A paradox indeed!

We are mistaken in thinking that our eyes enable us to see the true reality. Rav Shimon also observed with his eyes and prayed, but prayer did not impose the same restrictions on him that it imposes on most people. Prayer limits what the soul previously experienced, because just as with the eye, a restriction must be imposed on the potential in order for the soul to discover Light in the physical reality.

On the first day of *Rosh Hashanah*, the soul has already ascended to the World of Formation, beyond the boundaries of Satan's influence. But the physical reality must continue to exist—for without this reality, and without the assisting device called prayer, we cannot manifest the revelation of the 99%. When one prays, a diminution of previous spiritual achievement is created. Therefore, perhaps it is best that we do not pray at all. Again, this is a paradox: Without sight, nothing can be revealed, and everything is forced to remain in a potential state. As long as we are in the World of Action, nothing will be achieved through the ascent of the soul's consciousness alone.

Upon examining the senses, we find that sight is even more limited than smell, for the sense of smell reports the presence of one substance or another. One may, for example, readily discern the smoke of a fire from the smell of a steak. But on the retina, the eye displays an upside-down image of reality; it depicts things in a state that runs counter to their actual being. Therefore, the eye is subject to an even more serious limitation than the nose. A certain restriction applies on the first day of *Rosh Hashanah* because the body has not yet joined the spiritual consciousness of the soul. At this point, the eye and all other aspects of one's physical nature remain in their lowest state. This is also an advantage, however; it is a step downward and at the same time a step upward. The restriction on the first day is that there is no ascent of the physical reality; everything we see, hear, smell, taste, and feel has undergone no spiritual ascent. But when *Malchut* is in its most physical state, it is also in a state in which the potential revelation of Light is the greatest. So the aspect of restriction is at the same time more revealing. The greater the restriction, the greater the revelation.

When we do not see minute details, we are able to see the complete picture in our broad field of vision. The best means by which we can attain total perspective is by constantly and rapidly moving back and forth, zooming in and out before each angle of vision has time to impose its limitations on us. Then we never quite see a concrete image. At the moment we see a certain image, we have already imposed a restriction upon ourselves. Before that, we have seen more. Thus, the first day of *Rosh Hashanah* is a day of harsh judgment because it is without the ascent of the body—and without *Malchut*, nothing can be revealed. Returning to our metaphor, it is like a stone that is thrown into a lake and intercepted by a passing boat. Since the stone will never hit the water, the concentric waves that potentially began to form will never be realized. The first day is connected to the left column—to Cain, or harsh judgment. In a certain sense, the physical reality does not impose restrictions. It does not reveal a thing, but at the same time it has no restriction.

Now we have a much broader and clearer understanding of this issue. On the first day of *Rosh Hashanah*, a person feels unfocused inner sensations related to misdeeds that he has committed during the year, but he will never know or experience the full extent of their effects. Let us assume, for example, that we have committed an offense against a man who owns many factories, and as a result the man has decided to retire from his business and close those factories. On a physical level we have offended only one person, but on the 99% level we have caused thousands of other people to become unemployed, each of whom has a family. The concentric waves of our actions reach dimensions so vast that we are unable to imagine them.

This is exactly what we are feeling and the way we are judged on the first day of *Rosh Hashanah*—for on that day we are not limited by the 1% reality. Therefore, this day is one of harsh judgment. On this day we do not see anything specific, and because of this we are no longer restricted to the person we offended directly. On this day there is no spiritual ascent of the physical perception. Consequently, no intellectual restriction on the spiritual perception applies, and we may connect to the full scope of the consequences of our actions from the past year. In a sense, each negative action—every action that causes grief or damage to others or to the environment—attracts Light to the world without advance preparation of an appropriate vessel for the revelation and containment of that Light.

The attraction of Light is referred to by the code word *"Gvurot"* (power, might), and the unrestrained way in which the Light must be revealed is referred to by the code word judgment. When there is no suitable vessel for containing and revealing the Light in a balanced manner, it is manifested in the form of damage or a sorrowful event. Since the entire universe is connected by quantum energy, every judgment and *Gvurah* adversely affects the entire world unless it is restricted and balanced.

In order that we may deal with the unbalanced energy we have attracted during the year by means our actions, intentional or otherwise, the *Gvurot* must be balanced and the judgments restricted. This may be accomplished through the blowing of the *Shofar*, when performed in a certain procedure and with certain meditations as taught by Rav Shimon Bar Yochai and The Ari.

Rosh Hashanah falls in the seventh month. Is this when the world was created? Actually, the world was created five days before *Rosh Hashanah*! The Ari and *The Zohar* reveal that it was on *Rosh Hashanah* that the first human being was born. Therefore, we celebrate the birthday of man on that day. In this sense, all human beings should celebrate *Rosh Hashanah*, for we are all sparks of that first man's breath, and therefore this day is a common birthday shared by us all. If this is so, let us erase from our minds, at least for the time being, the thought that some connection exists between the creation of the world and *Rosh Hashanah*. And let us now replace that thought with a clear understanding of the connection between *Rosh Hashanah* and the origin of the human species.

What occurred on that day of origin? The Ari explains clearly that on the day the first man was created, which is the sixth day, man sinned—and many other things happened as well. On this day, man "fell" and was banished from the Garden of Eden as punishment for his sin. But on this day we all fell; we all participated in the sin because we were all there, contained within Adam's soul. As a result, the fall of the first man led to the fall of the entire world. Kabbalah tells us that Adam's height before the Sin was 100 feet. Since the fall of Adam, however, all the creatures of the world—including man—have proportionally diminished in size. The entire balance of the universe has been changed, and all creatures have become dwarfed in the same proportion. Furthermore, some creatures have become rare but not extinct. In every generation, at least one male and one female of each class and species of animal and plant continues to exist until this day. Nothing has disappeared or become extinct since Creation. Preservationists claim that unless certain precautionary measures are taken, some species are doomed to vanish from the earth—but there is no proof to support their claims. This is a basic teaching of Kabbalah.

On the day of Adam's fall, we all fell. Not only did we fall in our physical dimensions, but we fell from our spiritual dimension as well.

In what way do spiritual essence and physical essence differ? In Genesis 1:27 it is written, "And God created man in His own image, in the image of God He created him; male and female created He them." All this took place on the sixth day of Creation, which is *Rosh Hashanah*, the first day of *Tishrei*. Genesis 1 describes the creation of the World of Truth, the 99% reality. When we refer to male and female, we are therefore referring to male and female aspects such as the Light and the Vessel rather than Adam and Eve—who, as described in Genesis 2, were created out of dust.

Genesis, Chapter 2:21 reads, "And Hashem, God caused a deep sleep to fall upon the man, and he slept; and He took one of his ribs, and closed up the place with flesh instead thereof." But did the Creator really act according to hospital operating room procedures? Could He not have created Eve without anesthetizing and operating on Adam? Or did Adam undergo an experience in which the female aspect of his body was removed, after which this aspect realized itself within a second body? Truthfully, on *Rosh Hashanah* many of us undergo a similar experience in which the soul leaves the body, although most of us are unaware of it. In point of fact, during sleep we temporarily leave the body each night in order to rest and replenish ourselves for the next day.

When a person feels fatigued, what exactly is it that has tired? The soul does not tire, nor do the atoms. Fatigue, like other limitations of the physical body, is an expression of the body's desire to receive. This limitation does not, however, limit the inner quality of man. When Rav Akiva felt hunger, he would say to his body, "Go eat, and when you have eaten enough, let me know. In the meantime, I will watch you from the side and busy myself with other things." The "I" who spoke to the body was connected to the Tree of Life.

The Zohar explains that man has two bodies: one that is spiritual and connected to the Tree of Life, and another that is physical and connected to the illusion of limitation, restriction, and disease. During sleep, the soul is released from the restrictions of physical desire, and in this state of freedom, it can recharge and refresh itself with energy from the 99% realm. Sleep therefore liberates both the soul and the body. At the time the world was created, all the tools man required to win the battle against the negative forces were created as well. The reason man has not won this battle lies in the fact that he is unaware of these tools and has yet to make use of them.

Sawing (*nesirah*) is a term used to describe a spiritual experience in physical terms—specifically, the experience of the soul leaving the body. To clarify this concept, let us consider the example of clinical death. Imagine a man who is undergoing major surgery. Suddenly the monitoring devices beside him indicate that he has ceased to breathe, that his heart has stopped beating, and that his brain-wave activity has flattened. From a medical standpoint, the person is clinically dead—and after ten minutes, the medical staff is prepared to cease their efforts to revive him. But just then, the man inexplicably returns to life.

Upon awakening, the man tells the medical staff all that had transpired in the room around him during the time he was supposedly dead. He tells the doctors exactly where each of them had stood and what each had said. But how could he have heard these conversations and seen all that was going on around him when his eyes were closed and his brain was void of all activity? From a kabbalistic perspective, we know that for this ten-minute period, the soul and inner qualities of this man's body had simply left his physical body, which is both restricting and restricted. The soul thus saw and heard all that was taking place in a direct fashion, unrestrained by the inhibitions imposed by the five senses. This is the only true explanation for so-called near-death experiences—which are actually experiences of death itself.

The true spiritual body is as transparent as the wind. The soul and the spiritual body can shed their physical body. This action, in which the inner quality separates from the exterior, is called "Sawing". And it is this, rather than the *Shofar* or the prayers, that is the true focal point of *Rosh Hashanah*. Everything else is simply a means of achieving Sawing.

Through Sawing we are able to detach ourselves from our bodies, for both the body and its sins are connected to each other by the desire to receive for the self alone. The physical body of the man who has sinned must somehow undergo a process of death. The issue here is not reward and punishment, but rather cause and effect. If a man has stolen or committed murder, he must pay for his actions—whether by slow death, which may last for 30 years, or by immediate death. Regardless of how it expresses itself, the principle of reward and punishment must be realized.

According to kabbalistic teaching, when Satan stands before the Supernal Courts and enumerates a person's sins, he looks down and sees that person's body cast away without life, for its soul and inner quality have left it during the process of Sawing. But if this is true, what is the point of judging a dead man? The reason is that once this viewing takes place, Satan withdraws, disregards the man, and moves on to the next case.

Thus, The Ari explains that in order to be saved on the Day of Judgment, we must undergo the process of Sawing. This, specifically, is what all the prayers, the blowing of the *Shofar*, and the special intentions are for. In Sawing, we separate our true inner quality from our external body. This body was once devoid of all consciousness, from the time of Creation until man's first "bite" of the Tree of Knowledge of Good and Evil. The body then began to disrupt and limit the soul's internal quality. Every sense of lack that we experience—be it in health, finance, or relationships—arises completely from the blockage of the Light by the physical body. The "forbidden fruit" was the perfect representation of the connection between Adam's body and the consciousness of the Tree of Knowledge of Good and Evil. The tree itself is not evil, but its consciousness creates evil in the man who connects to it.

The principle of Sawing was established by the Creator at the time of Creation. The conventional understanding of *Rosh Hashanah* holds that when people ask the Creator for forgiveness on this day, the Creator forgives them their sins and then continues on his way. As we have seen, however, this is not an accurate interpretation of the holiday, since mere "forgiveness" is never sufficient to the task of rectifying our mistakes. Just as environmental pollution continues to sully the atmosphere even after a smokestack has been shut down, so too do our transgressions continue to pollute the universe with negativity. Industrial sewage and smoke are nothing more than a result of inconsiderate, unrestrained, and unbalanced planning stemming from the desire to receive on the part of entrepreneurs and factory owners. The pollution that results from evil intent and egocentricity is no less important. These acts of pollution are judged on *Rosh Hashanah*.

So why come to the war room to pray or to listen to the *Shofar*? We have heard that the *Shofar* stuns Satan and blurs his senses. But how does it do so? Does the sound of the *Shofar* hit him like a blow of the fist? And if so, what happens if the blowing is not strong? The answer is that the *Shofar* confuses Satan not by hitting him, but by Sawing off our physical body so that Satan is fooled into thinking that the body is no more than a corpse, the affairs of which are no longer worthy of discussion in the Upper Courts.

We are compelled to bear the consequences of environmental pollution, for example, which according to *The Zohar* is nothing more than a result of lack of consideration on the part of man toward his fellow man. A person who builds a factory that pollutes the air must halt that factory's activity or install a means of preventing the pollution—and if he does not do so of his own accord, the government will compel him to. As a result of the principle of reflection, he who pollutes his environment is liable to breathe polluted air, and he who behaves in a considerate manner is liable to breathe clean air. But if the entire planet becomes polluted, how will this cosmic principle exist? The answer is to be found in the principle of Sawing, which separates the boys from the men, the inconsiderate from the considerate. Without Sawing, there would also be no chance for the polluter to disconnect from the physical reality of reaction—a reality according to which he is doomed to breathe polluted air.

Although we might wish to believe that our actions have no reaction, we are taught by the Sages and by the Torah that the Day of Judgment comes once a year—and on that day, all the evil intents we have accumulated are enumerated, and our account is settled.

Any action is a cause and is therefore connected to *Zeir Anpin*, while any reaction is an effect and is connected to *Malchut*. When a man gives to charity or tithes, he is Sawing a bit of *Malchut* off himself. As a result, he is reducing the physical reaction to which he is subject as a result of his actions. It can thus be seen that charity literally saves us from death. This is what happens on *Rosh Hashanah* as well, when Sawing applies to all human beings throughout the world—and when everyone is given an opportunity to separate from the negativity they have accumulated over the year. The Ari says that the negativity we have caused and turned into part of the universe may be separated from us by Sawing so that the righteous will not have to suffer the consequences of the wicked's actions. Were it not for the mechanism of Sawing, the righteous would perish along with the wicked.

Each year, the validity of Sawing is renewed. The right-eous connect to *Zeir Anpin*, beyond the physical reality, and are spared the misfortunes that will plague the physical world in the coming year. Sawing allows for a separation between the poten-tial state and the result—that is, a separation between *Zeir Anpin* and *Malchut*. This means that even if the entire world were pol-luted and there were only one righteous man, that one man would be able to separate himself from the pollution and would not be affected by it or by the severe judgment that it draws to the world. If the pollution were absolute physical and spiritual reality, and if there were no Sawing in the world, there would be no way to eliminate it, and the *Shofar* would be of no use.

In order to attend to the problem, however, one must first be detached from it, just as a psychologist must be detached from his patients' neuroses in order to view them objectively. And in order to be detached, one needs Sawing. On *Rosh Hashanah* the physical reality, in which all problems are found, is separated from the spiritual reality of *Zeir Anpin*, and in this way we are separated from the pollution that has been created in the world. In this situation, says the Talmud, the righteous are immediately inscribed in the Book of Life—that is to say, they will not be affected by the negativity caused by others. But what about the negativity caused by individuals? How are individuals to disconnect from negativity? Will it suffice to beg the Creator for forgiveness? And does the blowing of the *Shofar* guarantee such forgiveness?

Consider this example. If an employer fires a worker from his factory and that worker commits suicide as a result, will begging forgiveness on *Rosh Hashanah* return the deceased to his family? Can the owner of the factory who fired the employee claim that he did so in order to help that employee as part of his *tikkun?* On no account is this the case. Nevertheless, if the blowing of the *Shofar* is performed with the correct meditations, it can in fact enable the factory owner to perform the act of *Teshuvah* and thereby rectify his error at its very root—and at the same time receive protection from judgment for the entire year. The blowing of the *Shofar* reduces the judgment and banishes the prosecutor (Satan) from the Upper Courts.

There are two stages in this process. The first stage is sleep—detachment from the daily reality, resting the 4% of the brain that is active in the wakeful state. The second stage is deep sleep, which is an ascent to another level of consciousness—such as the ascent of the soul to *Binah*, which lies far from ordinary consciousness, for charging and renewal. With regard to this matter, we must remember that such an ascent of the soul takes place only during the nighttime hours. As a result, daytime sleep is not as refreshing as nighttime sleep. For the same reason, it is recommended that one undergo surgery under full anesthesia during nighttime hours, because there will then be a place for the soul, which can subsequently be received and charged by the time the anesthetics wear off.

The Ari says, *"Zeir Anpin* goes to sleep." Why? Male and female were created on the sixth day, back to back. In this situation there is no flow of energy, no revelation of Light, and no grip for negativity. This is how all babies come into the world as well—because if it were not so, the *Klipot* (shells of negativity) would take hold of them at the moment of their birth, and the babies would stand no chance of surviving. After Adam fell into a deep sleep, Sawing was performed with the objective of changing this and bringing Adam and Eve to a state of harmonic communication, face to face. Were it not for the Sin, the unification would have taken place on Shabbat, on which day protection is afforded from *Klipot*. As a result of the Sin, however, the coupling was pushed up to a weekday and was performed in the presence of *Klipot*, which fed off of it. The issue of anesthesia before surgery was intended to allow for the separation of the patient's male and female aspects. Pain belongs exclusively to the female aspect, to the physical body. The anesthesia therefore works only on *Zeir Anpin*, the male aspect, which is connected to consciousness. Because the male aspect is separated from body consciousness by the anesthesia, the patient does not feel the physical pain. The female aspect feels pain during the operation, but since it is not connected to the consciousness, this is not enough to cause the patient pain. Nor does the brain feel pain when operated on; the pain comes only from the incision of the skin and the Sawing of the head—for the brain is connected to *Keter*, and *Keter* belongs to the Light, not to the Vessel. Seeing that this is so, the brain does not feel pain or, for that matter, any other physical sensation originating in it.

Why, then, were *Zeir Anpin* consciousness (Adam) and *Malchut* consciousness (Eve) attached to one another, back to back, when they were created?

Judgment means immediate and uncontrolled uncovering of the Light, not a gradual flow. The Light is in all places at all times. A connection to the Light creates a lightbulb filament within us—an element that applies a force of resistance, thereby allowing for the closing of the circuit and for the controlled flow of Light through us. When a person sins, he creates judgment in the back of his male aspect and stops the flow of Light through himself because he has not applied a force of resistance and hence has not created any reflecting Light.

These judgments are unchanneled and uncontrolled energy. The difference between a normal cell and a cancerous one lies in the fact that the cancerous cell is animated by uncontrolled energy of judgment. And it is just such judgments that must be sawed off on *Rosh Hashanah*. Toward this goal, when the moon is in covering, our male aspect falls into a deep sleep and spiritual "surgery" takes place. During this operation, the energy of judgment is transferred from the male to the female aspect.

How do we free ourselves from the hold of the negative forces? Through a form of spiritual anesthesia. On the first day of *Rosh Hashanah*, *Zeir Anpin* falls into a deep sleep. At this time, the supply of Light to the physical body ceases, and the judgments that have attached to the body during the past year are sawed away. The judgments then drop off and continue to hold on to the Light remaining in the feminine aspect.

The separation of Eve from Adam describes the exact process that takes place in each of us on *Rosh Hashanah*. The Ari explains that the words "and closed up the place with flesh instead thereof" are a code describing the substitution of mercy for judgment. The more merciful acts we perform, the larger

will be our spiritual Vessel, and the greater the revelation of
Light that will be enabled.

In the treatment of cancer, tissue is usually surgically
removed, and adjacent cells—both malignant and healthy—are
subsequently destroyed by means of chemotherapy. The surgi-
cal stage of this treatment corresponds to the Sawing on *Rosh
Hashanah*, and the therapeutic stage to the action of the *Shofar*.
The sawing of the judgments implies their restriction and transformation into a harmless form. The judgments do not disappear, because the Light never disappears—but they do change
form, passing from an aggressive to a passive state.

On *Rosh Hashanah*, there is an accumulation of judgments
as a result of the negative actions we performed during the year.
We have described how, on the first day of *Rosh Hashanah*, *Zeir
Anpin* (Adam) fell into a deep sleep. On this day, the Creator
similarly puts the *Zeir Anpin* aspect in each of us to sleep. When
we were born, the male and female aspects in us were back to
back. Had this not been so, the external forces would have
sucked all the Light that flowed through us. *Rosh Hashanah* is a
blessing because we now return to the state of our birth, when
no Light flowed through us and we were free from negativity.

After *Zeir Anpin* is put to sleep, the Creator performs
spiritual surgery on us, removing the judgments from the male
aspect within us and transferring them to the female aspect.
This is the interpretation of the coded biblical description that
says, "And the rib . . . made He [a woman]." After the removal
of the judgments, the Creator fills their place with mercy—for

mercy is the natural consequence of the lack of judgment. Mercy is the vessel through which the Light of Wisdom can flow and be revealed in a controlled and balanced manner.

Upon the birth of the first man, the Creator had to devise a solution to a problem that had not yet arisen: that of the Original Sin. The Creator provided a solution in advance by giving man free will, indicating that He knew man might sin. Man was created with free will so that he would be able to remove his Bread of Shame. The condition that solved the problem in advance lay in the division of man into male and female, into internal and external aspects, so that Sawing could take place between them.

The side connected to the power of Light, the home of the soul, is that which falls asleep. Why?

Judgment is an accumulation of all energies that can form a script of disorder for the year to come. On *Rosh Hashanah*, our objective is to reduce the judgment—to numb its sting. And one way to achieve this is by Sawing judgment acts on the physical level, and if we disconnect ourselves from this level, we are not affected by judgment at all.

As we know, the sun gives light to the moon. So, too, does man feed off the Light that comes from *Zeir Anpin*. On the physical level, *Zeir Anpin* is represented by the sun. The physical body, which is *Malchut*, lacks any Light of its own. The soul in relation to the body is like *Zeir Anpin* in relation to *Malchut*. Yet this issue must be further explained, for understanding it can strengthen our connection to the process as a whole. All the sins we have committed have created energies that may draw and bring judgment on us—judgment that can come to us straight from *Binah* or, alternatively, through *Zeir Anpin*, which receives all its Light and strength from *Binah*. Each year, on *Rosh Hashanah*, all people go back in time and for a moment experience the same process that Adam underwent. The eye does not see this, just as it does not perceive that once every seven years our entire body undergoes complete regeneration. But the fact that the eye does not see things does not mean that they do not take place.

On *Rosh Hashanah*, we return to the state in which the soul and the body are back to back, and there is no flow of energy between them. This means that we are dead, just like the operating room patient we previously described. In this state, negativity no longer holds sway over us and is Sawed away. When we are born, the soul and the body are in a similar back-to-back state, and the power of the Creator Saws and separates them. When the body is disconnected from *Zeir Anpin*, *Zeir Anpin* is given the opportunity to connect directly to *Binah*. At the same time, all the judgments that were connected to and dropped off *Zeir Anpin* now concentrate in *Malchut*. The Sawing off of the judgments from the back of *Zeir Anpin* and their subsequent transfer to *Malchut* are both performed when *Zeir Anpin* is in a deep sleep.

The relation between *Zeir Anpin* and *Malchut* is similar to that between a man and a woman, or between the sun and the moon. Outer space, although flooded with the sun's rays, is totally dark; it is only when sunlight hits the moon that the moon become apparent. In much the same manner, *Malchut* allows for the uncovering of the potential that is hidden in *Zeir Anpin*. When all the judgments are concentrated in *Malchut*, the physical body pays for all its sins against *Binah*. Simultaneously, the spiritual body, which is dissociated from the physical body, feeds directly off *Binah*. This dissociation is the Sawing, which is described in the biblical code as a sleep that descended on our male aspect—on *Zeir Anpin*, on Adam—just like the Sawing off of our soul when we fall asleep.

This, then, is the explanation of the description of deep sleep that fell upon Adam in the Garden of Eden. Without this explanation, the Sawing would no longer be a logical part of the biblical story. The rib is a code name for judgment, and Eve is *Malchut*. When Sawing takes place on us, we are separated from the consciousness that feeds us, from our own private *Zeir Anpin*—which feeds not only our physical body, but our soul and the inner qualities of our body as well.

The purpose of the *Shofar* is to reduce the judgments that have been concentrated in *Malchut*, and its action is carried out by means of the meditations. While the *Shofar* reduces the *Dinim* (judgments), it also awakens *Zeir Anpin* from its deep sleep. The Sawing separates *Zeir Anpin*, the cause, from *Malchut*, the effect. As has been discussed, it is known that the cause influences the effect, but that the effect cannot influence its cause. Were it not for the Sawing, the lists of judgments in *Zeir Anpin* could not have been reduced by any activity on the part of *Malchut*. But after *Zeir Anpin* falls into a deep sleep—and after the judgments are transferred from it to *Malchut*—these judgments can in fact be reduced through actions performed within the limits of *Malchut*: the blowing of the *Shofar* and the meditations. These activities act, in effect, as a kind of spiritual surgery; the *Shofar* cleans our "behavioral chart" and transforms the sins written on it into virtues. These virtues are then included in the set of cosmic considerations that determine our life script for the new year. As has been discussed, we can go back in time and repair that which we have damaged in the past, including our actions in previous reincarnations. During the month of *Elul*, we perform the act of *Teshuvah*—we go back in time and correct our consciousness. Thus, when we reach *Rosh Hashanah*, past and present are one, consciousness has been rectified, and all that remains is the minimization of judgment by means of the *Shofar* and the meditations.

Following the minimization of judgment, *Zeir Anpin*—the soul that serves as home to the Creator's Light within us, the initiating part within us, the spark—reawakens. The reduced judgments now ascend to *Zeir Anpin*, so that by means of *Teshuvah* the damage caused in the victim's world may be repaired. This would be reflected, for example, in the resurrection of a murder victim. But such action requires that *Zeir Anpin* be awake, for *Malchut* is not able to accomplish it alone.

Scientists believe—and perhaps rightly so—that they can arrive at a cohesive description of the universe's first moments. The objective of this effort is to integrate the description of all the forces in the universe into a single mathematical framework. Perhaps cosmologists will make a dramatic discovery about the cosmos that will prove capable of explaining something about our universe.

But where does that leave those of us who are not scientific experts? Does it bring about the unity of mankind? A world without destruction and chaos? Clearly not. We cannot leave this work to the scientific community, as their day in court has come and gone. The time has thus come for the "man on the street" to wake up, act, and achieve the results for which mankind has been waiting thousands of years. The man on the street must now, of necessity, seize the bull by its horns.

If in fact we take the steps necessary on *Rosh Hashanah* to reorganize the universe—if we attack and destroy the tremendous negative human activity that has accumulated over hundreds of years—then and only then, says *The Zohar*, will we be able to bring all things to a renewed unity, the result of which will be a universe rooted in peace, serenity, and brotherhood.

From a kabbalistic standpoint, the action that must be taken to bring this about is not physical but metaphysical. Therefore, we must stop believing that technological developments will solve the problems of our lives. Instead, positive change must come from the mind, from the true reality of thought consciousness.

Kabbalah teaches that human beings once lived for 1,000 years. Later on, human life expectancy gradually dropped to a minimum of 36 years. Yet today life expectancy has risen again, to its current average of nearly 76 years. What has changed?

Physicians will, of course, say that this upward shift is a direct result of improved sanitation conditions and advances in health care delivery. But if this is the case, how can they explain the fact that today there are more sick people than ever, and that hospitals are constantly at maximum occupancy? The kabbalistic explanation for this recent increase in life expectancy is simply this: the phenomenon began when Israelites, en masse, started to read *The Zohar*.

In recent years it has been possible to find more and more people who have exceeded the age of 100 while remaining in good health and clarity of mind. A unique phenomenon is thus taking place throughout the world. By the end of the 21st century, there are expected to be more than one million such healthy citizens living in the United States alone. This phenomenon is a direct result of the increase in the number of people who, year after year, are restoring order to the universe through powerful guided prayer on *Rosh Hashanah*. And the more we persevere in this activity—the more people there are—the stronger the process will grow, and the greater will be its influence over those who remain in robotic awareness. We have reached the threshold of a new field of medicine—a new technology that could not be simpler or more accessible. This New Age medicine is based on the restoration of order and harmony to the universe by means of the knowledge hidden in the Torah and *The Zohar*.

As Rav Shimon said, "Only a fool does not ask questions." Religion was never intended to be robotic. It is therefore vital that we ask questions and work toward building a spiritual vessel. Our lives depend on these two days of *Rosh Hashanah*. We wish each other Happy New Year in order to remove from ourselves the chaos that is usually ordained to us on this day, but we will succeed in this effort only if we mean it and make it happen.

Each month we connect to the energy of the Ana Becho'ach through the letters of the month, but on *Rosh Hashanah* the letters of the month have no influence at all. All other months have both positive and negative aspects, but on *Rosh Hashanah* there is only the negative one. In the month of Tammuz (Cancer), for example, a cancerous disease may begin. But the sign of Cancer also has positive attributes, so through the Ana Becho'ach we can connect to those aspects and thereby avert the disease. Each month has both internal and external consciousness, body consciousness as well as soul consciousness. Similarly, the moon has a system composed of two parts: one offering us the positive attributes of the month, and the other helping us build a protective shield to deflect its negative implications. But this system may be weak or absent. If, for example, this happens in the month of Tammuz, then we will be exposed to the possibility of contracting cancer. If we know how to protect ourselves, however, we will not become sick, for we will have chosen to connect with the positive elements.

Negative energy is always accompanied by positive energy to counteract it—with the single exception of *Rosh Hashanah*. On *Rosh Hashanah*, there is only judgment and negative energy. On *Rosh Hashanah* our eyes do indeed see the moon, but its positive channel is concealed from us. This has to do with the sign of Libra. People born under this sign see both sides of an issue, but since they see both sides equally clearly, they have difficulty making decisions. This trait originates with the covering of the positive channel of the moon during the entrance of Libras into the physical world. Libras see the negative and positive sides in minute detail, but they lack a connection with positive energy. As a result, they are afraid of decisions. The negative and positive are balanced, but for them, the additional energy that would tip the scales in a positive direction does not exist.

Now we understand why Rav Shimon had to spend exactly three days with the prayer leader and the *Shofar* blower. In reality, it had nothing at all to do with their talents or cognitive abilities. To the contrary, Rav Shimon knew that the prayer leader and the *Shofar* blower needed to be nothing short of perfect. Like a missile-launching system that is composed of many parts, everything in this effort must be in perfect working order if it is to accomplish its task successfully. The prayer leader and the blower are also systems, each composed of separate components that must operate in unison. The three days with Rav Shimon teach us that the three aspects must be integrated so as to form a unity—right, left, and central. Rav Shimon purified the *Chazan* (prayer leader) and the *Shofar* blower, and this purity manifests an infinite flow of energy, creating the three-column system.

Just sitting together as a family will not accomplish this goal. But one family member doing the work of *Rosh Hashanah* in synagogue can indeed act as a spiritual insurance policy for the entire year—not only for that individual but also for his family and his business. Awareness and intention are essential elements

in this process. We must know what is happening. For it is only
by means of knowledge that will we achieve the objective of *Rosh
Hashanah*.

What is
YOM KIPPUR?

From *Rosh Hashanah*, we will now proceed to the next important cosmic event: *Yom Kippur*, the Day of Atonement. This day has been so widely misunderstood that many now neglect what was once the most important and sacred day of the entire year. Here we will deviate from the conventional belief that *Yom Kippur* is a day of forgiveness and pardon, as can be inferred from a literal translation of its name. Instead, through the teachings of Kabbalah, we will explore the more profound inner meaning of this holiday. By doing so, we hope to move the reader—and all of mankind—toward removal of the negative cosmic activity that for 2,000 years has seemed to be such an integral part of our lives. From here on, let things be completely different!

The Torah, in Leviticus 23:26, describes the holiday as follows:

How be it on the tenth day of this seventh month is the Day of Atonement; there shall be a holy convocation unto you; and you shall afflict your souls; and you shall bring an offering made by fire unto God. And you shall do no manner of work in that same day; for it is a Day of Atonement, to make atonement for you before Hashem your God. For whatsoever soul it be that does any manner of work in that same day, that soul will I destroy from among his people. You shall do no manner of work; it is a statute for ever throughout your generations in all your dwellings. It shall be unto you a Sabbath of solemn rest, and you shall afflict your souls; in the ninth day of the month at evening, from evening unto evening, shall you keep your Sabbath.

This is the essence of *Yom Kippur*. To be sure, there are many additional aspects of this sacred day, but these seem to have lost their relevance. They deal with the High Priest and with the offering of sacrifices. Traditionalists cannot address these issues beyond a vague attempt to convey the significance of The Temple and the sacrifices. Nor do we have an opportunity to participate individually in the offering of sacrifices—or so it would seem. From the moment we begin to grasp the kabbalistic meaning of *Yom Kippur*, however, we will have a very different perspective.

In order to understand the meaning of *Yom Kippur*, we
must remember that the kabbalistic holidays are not just celebrations or commemorations in the usual sense. The forces
of the universe reveal themselves during holidays. Therefore,
since *Yom Kippur* is mentioned in the Torah, we may understand that in the course of this day, a certain cosmic code is
revealed throughout the universe. This is the true meaning
of *Yom Kippur*.

But let us first discuss our physical circumstances,
which seem to trouble most people today. We need to gain
an understanding of our own bodies, for without such understanding we will not be able to move beyond them to our
internal, spiritual aspect. *Yom Kippur* is a day of fasting that
falls on the tenth day of *Tishrei*. It is the dramatic conclusion
of the Ten Days of Repentance that follow *Rosh Hashanah*,
and as such it is considered to be the most important day of
the year. This is the essence of the day, as it is understood by
those who observe tradition.

Now let us pose several daring questions that have
never likely been asked outside the realm of Kabbalah.

First, why was this day—the most sacred day of the
year—chosen to be celebrated on the tenth of *Tishrei*? Is this
significant? Why must *Yom Kippur* fall precisely on the tenth
day?

Second, what is the origin of the word Kippur (atonement)? It is widely believed that this term stems from the

Aramaic words *kapparah* (atonement or pardon) and *mechilah* (forgiveness). But for us, as students of Kabbalah, this is not sufficient.

Third, why must this holiday fall in the wake of *Rosh Hashanah*?

Fourth, why are five kinds of prohibitions associated with this day? The five prohibitions defined by the Sages for the purpose of afflicting the soul are as follows: (1) the prohibition against all eating and drinking; (2) the prohibition against bathing for the sake of pleasure; (3) the prohibition against anointing our bodies with lotions, oils, or cosmetics; (4) the prohibition against wearing leather shoes; and (5) the prohibition against sexual relations. The Torah further admonishes that those who do not observe these prohibitions will be excommunicated from the Nation of Israel. This is exceptionally severe. Moreover, these five prohibitions are the same as those practiced on the ninth day of *Av*. Why are these five prohibitions necessary, and how are they connected to the ninth day of *Av*?

Fifth, on *Yom Kippur* there are an exceptional number of prayer services to be recited—five, to be exact. But why five, as opposed to the customary three daily prayer services? It is even stranger that on the ninth day of the month of *Tishrei*—on the eve of *Yom Kippur*—the Talmud recommends that we eat as much as we can. The reason is that each act of eating performed on this day—no matter whether we have three, eight, or fourteen meals—represents an aspect of fasting. This is a rather strange concept: Although we eat and drink in excess, we are actually fasting.

The sixth "tradition" is perhaps the strangest of all. At morning's first light on the eve of *Yom Kippur*, kabbalists indulge in what is known as *Kapparot*—the slaughtering of a chicken for the expiation of judgments. Anyone who is sensitive to the issue of animal rights will surely cry out against this precept. Nevertheless, it too is part of the package deal that is called *Yom Kippur*. According to The Ari, this precept must be performed before the dawn of the ninth day of *Tishrei*. The significance of this ritual has to a great extent been lost and forgotten. Those who still practice the precept often slaughter the chicken on any of the days between *Rosh Hashanah* and *Yom Kippur*. Indeed, Many today prohibit this practice on the eve of *Yom Kippur* because the anticipated workload of those involved is too great; it is thought that sufficient care might not be taken in sharpening the blade of the knife, which according to Israelite law must be without defect. Therefore, in Israel today it is prohibited to perform the slaughtering on the first light of the eve of the ninth of Tishrei—and as a result, those who stubbornly persist in performing this Mitzvah are forced to do so on another day.

Finally, there is a certain practice associated with *Yom Kippur* that is zealously maintained by many secular people who do not otherwise practice. These people come to synagogue on the eve of *Yom Kippur* specifically for the purpose of hearing the "*Kol Nidrei*" prayer, which cancels all vows.

This is significant for several reasons. First, the prayer is written in Aramaic, so few if any such worshipers are likely to understand its content. Second, and even more important, what is so significant about canceling vows that it attracts people to a synagogue they rarely if ever attend during the rest of the year? What is the source of this tradition's power—a tradition that is not clear even to Israelites?

If the Torah is a document that is to be studied and understood, then we should not leave out even a single section in our discussions. After all, we are dealing with the laws of the universe, and we are doing so in an effort to end the suffering and unhappiness of mankind, which continue to plague us year after year. ""So with this in mind, let us consider the matter of animal sacrifice, however upsetting it may be to many people.

There is a passage in Leviticus 16 that describes the function of Aaron, the High Priest, on *Yom Kippur*. In verses 5-6, it is written:

And he shall take of the congregation of the children of Israel two he-goats for a sin offering, and one ram for a burnt offering. And Aaron shall present the bullock of the sin offering, which is for himself, and make atonement for himself, and for his house.

It is written in verse 7:

> And he shall take the two he-goats, and set
> them before the Lord at the door of the tent of
> meeting. And Aaron shall cast lots upon the two
> he-goats: one lot for the Lord, and the other lot
> for Azazel. And Aaron shall present the he-goat
> upon which the lot fell for the Lord, and offer
> him for a sin offering. But the he-goat, on which
> the lot fell for Azazel, shall be set alive before the
> Lord, to make atonement over him, to send him
> away for Azazel into the wilderness.

How can the slaughtering and burning of animals
atone for the sins of Aaron and his household? Atonement is
clearly a major element of *Yom Kippur*. It is written in Leviticus
16 in Verse 21:

> And Aaron shall lay both his hands upon
> the head of the live he-goat, and confess over
> him all the iniquities of the children of Israel,
> and all their transgressions, even all their sins;
> and he shall put them upon the head of the he-
> goat, and shall send him away by the hand of an
> appointed man into the wilderness.

Why must we maintain these traditions today, when
The Temple no longer exists and the High Priest is no longer
active? Questions like these must be posed in the name of
reason, as well as in the name of authentic spiritual practice.

There is, after all, no prohibition against the posing of questions, and there has never been a law against knowledge and understanding. To the contrary, God must be known. The portion of Bo, in the Book of Exodus 10:2, declares, "You may know that I am Hashem." But he who does not ask questions shall never know.

Can one imagine this? By using both hands, the agreement of God is obtained. *The Zohar* explains that this means all sins will remain on the he-goat alone.

Rav Abba asked Rav Shimon three questions: Why must the ceremony be performed in the said manner? Why must the priest place his hands on the head of the he-goat? And why must all this take place on *Yom Kippur* and not on any other day? Rav Shimon replied that the purpose of these sacrifices is not for the purpose of pleasing God or for the benefit of any other metaphysical entity. To understand this, let us go back to the basic question: Why was *Yom Kippur* chosen to be the important holiday that falls on the tenth of Tishrei?

Has anyone ever asked why the entire world counts according to the base of ten? From a kabbalistic perspective, each time we encounter the number ten, we are dealing with completion. When we directly attacked and destroyed negative human consciousness on *Rosh Hashanah*, we dealt with one aspect on the first day. But if we are to achieve complete annihilation of the forces of negativity and death, we need more than one day. And for those who are not well versed in this issue, the meaning of a "day" is not merely a period of time but also an energy framework—an energy package sealed in a metaphysical bottle.

Each complete spiritual system is composed of ten aspects, also known as the Ten Sfirot. On the first day of *Rosh Hashanah*, we discuss *Keter*—the first *Sfirah*, the warhead of the missile. Then, on each subsequent day, yet another aspect of negative consciousness is revealed as part of our mission to combat chaos and negativity. Each of the Ten Days of Repentance thus represents a different *Sfirah* that we purge—a different package of negative energy that we must combat. It is as if the missile against which we launch our intercepting antimissile is made up of ten different parts, from its tip to its tail, which we must attack and destroy, one after the other.

When we asked why *Yom Kippur* was ordained to fall on the tenth of Tishrei, we were suggesting that this date was not set arbitrarily. *Yom Kippur* is the essence of the tenth of Tishrei. It is not, as one may mistakenly think, that *Yom Kippur* has given context to the date; *Yom Kippur* is simply the result of our success in the mission to destroy all parts of Satan's missile—a battle that lasts for ten consecutive days.

Put another way, you cannot simply enter the synagogue, listen to the Kol Nidrei prayer, and think that by doing so you have achieved your objective. You cannot arrive on *Yom Kippur* and say to God, "Forgive me, grant me pardon, and accept my atonement." That is not how it works. Instead, there are ten consecutive days of battle that must be waged. And on each day we must destroy a different part—a different *Sfirah*—of Satan's missile.

It is for this reason that the days between *Rosh Hashanah* and *Yom Kippur* are called the Ten Days of Repentance. On the third day of Tishrei and of Repentance, for example, all our prayers will be aimed at attacking and destroying the aspect of *Binah* in the missile of negativity. But, here again, there are ten different aspects that must be discussed, understood, and destroyed. And our prayers are the channels of communication that conduct the energy with which chaos will ultimately be destroyed. Throughout the first ten days of Tishrei—including *Yom Kippur*—we are in fact destroying all ten aspects of Satan's missile, one aspect per day, on both a physical and a spiritual level.

"But The Temple no longer exists in physical form," one might respond. Does this mean that we cannot succeed in our task? Does it mean that the energy of *Yom Kippur*, given to us by the Torah, is incomplete? If we can perform only part of the connection, can we then expect to achieve only part of the hoped-for result? And if so, how can we talk of complete atonement on *Yom Kippur*?

Rav Isaac Luria, The Ari, did not write Gate of Reincarnation in vain. He knew that when the entire public was one soul with him, it would be like placing both his hands on the head of the he-goat—the High Priest could atone for everyone's sins. So today, we too can realize atonement. But at the same time, we must ask some questions.

First, what really is atonement? And second, how does it take place? Does atonement mean that we have been bad children and are now asking for pardon and forgiveness? Can't we be forgiven all year round, on any day of the year? And even more significantly, could someone ask forgiveness and then carry on sinning as usual, with no change? Actually, this is how most people in the world understand atonement. The ceremonies of *Yom Kippur* have been performed year after year since the Revelation on Mount Sinai 3,400 years ago. Yet how many of us, over the years, have seen a change in the genetic code of the universe? How many among us can testify that their past year has been composed only of peace, tranquillity, health, success, happiness, and prosperity? All of mankind continues to suffer, and no hope for change seems to be in the offing. Let us therefore recognize the stark contrast between our participation in synagogue ceremonies year after year, and the lack of improvement and control we have seen in our lives.

To be sure, I do not wish to dissuade anyone from continuing to visit the synagogue or from continuing to pray or perform precepts. But how much have we, as human beings living in the universe, advanced as a result of this activity? When we begin to recognize the incompleteness of our *Yom Kippur* observance, we can at least begin to understand why *Yom Kippur* falls on the tenth day of the month of Tishrei. *Yom Kippur* is intended to remove all chaos from our lives. But if we fail to completely remove negative consciousness, then whatever we fail to remove will be included in the genetic code of our lives for the next year.

Preparations for Yom Kippur

No matter how diligently we may conduct ourselves on Yom Kippur, if there remains a single person to whom we have been unjust—if there is anyone who still hates us, or if any anger has gone unreconciled—we will not have succeeded. Even though God forgives all sins between man and God, and even though He pardons all the negative energy man has injected into the vast expanse of the universe, God cannot forgive transgressions between one person and another. Forgiveness must therefore come from the victim. A person can freely enter any synagogue, any church, any mosque, or any temple, and he may open a prayer book and pray without interruption; God will not disturb him. In the same manner, one may ceaselessly talk to the Creator. But the basic problem will remain between human beings. The main source of negative energy, more than any sin between man and God, will remain the desire to receive for the self alone.

Yom Kippur (translated as "a day like Purim") contains a connection to Purim consciousness—the consciousness of "love your neighbor as yourself," which is the key to a connection with *Binah*. This consciousness is the exclusive channel of communication that enables all other essential communications required on Yom Kippur. The connection to "love your neighbor as yourself" is like the connection to *Binah* itself.

In the holiday prayer book, we find many confessions. What is their meaning? During the Ten Days of Repentance, we regret and express our sorrow for sins we have committed in the course of the year. But is this enough? If I step on someone's foot and ask for forgiveness, does that make the pain go away? The entire concept of regret must be closely examined with the objective of reaching focused, practical, and meaningful conclusions. Put simply, regret does not equal confession. If I cause someone pain and am willing to experience the pain and sorrow I have caused, then from a kabbalistic standpoint there is only one way to rectify that which requires rectifying—and that is to return in consciousness to the time and place where the negative act was committed and, having done so, nullify the mistake at its inception. But if the act is over and the damage has been done, is this possible? How can we go back in time and rectify a mistake so that the victim no longer feels the pain?

Suppose I am rushing to a meeting and am so preoccupied that I do not notice a man standing in front of me on the street, and I inadvertently step on his foot. I immediately say to him, "I'm sorry, it was an accident." In this example, there was no intention on my part to hurt the man. And here we arrive at a lesson in Kabbalah that identifies with modern thought in the area of quantum theory.

When the physical expression of stepping on the foot occurred and we said it was unintentional, what exactly did we mean? In the narrow framework of the 1% world, we meant that there was a lack of malicious intent on our part. But what about the remaining 99%? Was I in control of my consciousness in all matters pertaining to my stepping on that foot? The answer is probably not. Because I was totally preoccupied with the meeting, from a kabbalistic perspective I had already determined my readiness to step on whoever might be in my way. At that moment, the desire to receive for myself alone rose above any other consideration in my mind. So the action of stepping on that person's foot did not begin the moment I walked past him, but rather much earlier—perhaps even before I began thinking of my meeting.

Could there have been another occurrence that brought about the "accident"—something involving my thought energy, a thought of desire to receive for myself alone? As for my "victim," there is no question that he had to be stepped on by somebody or something, as a past thought or action must have brought this result upon him. He must surely have deserved it, for nothing negative ever happens to us without cause. Seemingly negative occurrences are in fact the results of our desire to receive for ourselves alone.

The only thing left for me to do, then, is to distance myself from the act of trampling. That specific person was destined to be trod on. But why did I, of all people, have to execute the act? Or in yet another example, why did I, of all people, have to be involved in an accident in which a pedestrian was inadvertently run over? To be sure, this pedestrian was run over as a result of his desire to receive for himself, which was expressed at an earlier time—perhaps even in a previous reincarnation. Since the victim did not do a thing to change the genetic code of his cassette, he had no choice but to experience this event. But how was I chosen as the person to run him over? It must be because my consciousness corresponds with the consciousness that brought the injury upon the victim. I am the person who will have to suffer a guilty conscience as a result of having inadvertently hurt the pedestrian. The lack of intent to run over existed only within the 1%. From the quantum perspective, even if I acted out of an impulse of a desire to receive for myself three years ago, that would be sufficient to cause involvement in such an accident three years later—for the quantum connects events above and beyond the illusory dimension of time.

One of the easiest ways to nullify the desire to receive for ourselves is to sit quietly for a moment and isolate the specific desire that caused any accident, sorrow, or suffering we have inflicted on others. Responsibility must be taken for events, and we must decide to prevent their recurrence by destroying and canceling the desire that caused them. The moment we make this decision, we attain an alternate level of consciousness. And this means that we have gone back in time and eradicated the event.

To be sure, these are challenging concepts. Nevertheless, at this time, in the Age of Aquarius, we must redirect our thoughts and become more aware of our inner selves—our personal 99%. People who act within the 1% realm have lost all contact with their own essence. They have no real self-control, for our true and causative self lies in the 99% realm. This perspective may well seem revolutionary to many people, but it is one that we must begin to accept. Science understood it theoretically years ago, and this is a full, dramatic demonstration of the same cosmic principle.

The application of the quantum principle to the examples cited above—the foot treading and the car accident—reveals a single solution that is relevant to both. In short, we must distance ourselves from the physical expression of the event that caused another human sorrow or suffering. But is this possible? According to Kabbalah, the answer is yes—if we make the effort to go back in time. On a physical level, of course, this seems difficult to accomplish. How can we return in time and change things that have already become manifest in the physical realm?

Yet time travel is very real within the 99% realm. When we go back in time, we enter a different domain. And while moving through time, the spiritual identity of the traveler—the 99%—changes as well. The self that travels through time is not the same self that set out on this journey. The self that drove the car three years ago and caused the accident is not the same self that is returning in time today as part of the process of Repentance. The consciousness of the offending driver was bent on the desire to receive for the self alone, while the consciousness of Repentance is rooted in concern for our fellow man.

Kabbalah asserts that our entire physical reality is an illusion, from beginning to end. The idea that some things are subject to change while others are fixed in space and time is simply a fallacy. This fact, which enables us to act on different occasions out of different consciousness, is akin to the hallucinations of schizophrenia. Psychologists regard schizophrenia as a psychological disorder, but Kabbalah understands it very differently. We simply accept the change that person underwent—and even that the person himself changed to someone else.

True Repentance is possible only through the achievement of an alternate level of consciousness. And this requires real spiritual effort—effort that is directed at attacking and nullifying the desire to receive for the self alone and disconnecting it from our actions. This is the essence of the Ten Days of Repentance.

Through the holiday prayers composed by our Sages, we are able to realize time travel—to go "back to the future"—in order to identify and cancel the desire to receive for the self alone. The very attempt to gain control over the ego suffices to bring about a change in consciousness—provided, of course, that it is a true attempt rather than a temporary exercise aimed at deceiving the cosmic system. In this context, it should always be borne in mind that cosmic thought consciousness cannot be misled. At this level there are no facades, no illusions akin to those we might find in our physical reality. Anyone who considers deception a possibility should give it up here and now. One must make a real and honest attempt to effect change. And this is what takes place during the Ten Days of Repentance.

All the prohibitions, restrictions, and Mitzvot that we fulfill are nothing but convenient channels of communication that help us connect to the spiritual level of *Binah*. And this communication is our primary objective on Yom Kippur: we aim to arrive at the beginning of all time. Put another way, we are not aiming just to return to the moment before we caused another person pain, but also to return to a time long before that—to the actual moment of Creation. Again, this is a radical idea, but our objective is to get to the root of these matters in order to amend them at their source. Therefore, we must thoroughly and relentlessly investigate the cosmic code called Torah, which includes the concept of returning in time.

Unfortunately, we do not have the opportunity to go back in time every day. We can do this only once a year, on Yom Kippur. The Ten Days of Repentance embody the ten packets of energy that comprise the desire to receive for the self alone. More specifically, the ninth day is the most important period between *Rosh Hashanah* and Yom Kippur. The ninth day is related to *Yesod*. *Yesod* is the funnel for all eight previous energy packets, from *Keter* onward. It is the stem of all the potential energy that creates physical revelation in *Malchut*.

Action requires energy, and matter is a concentrated manifestation of energy. Kabbalah teaches that the foundation of all matter is not only energy, but also thought consciousness. This is an important point that is not always made clear.

We all are familiar with the problem of energy shortage, which affects not only nations but also individuals. Perhaps we may sometimes feel weak and fatigued, as if we have no strength to go on. Yet what we really lack is not physical energy, but rather thought consciousness. This is true not only for humans, but for machines and physical objects as well. They too are made up of atoms, which are in turn composed of pure energy. The thought consciousness that is the real basis of atoms and molecules directs all physical activity throughout the universe. And once we understand this by literally feeding ourselves with thought consciousness, we will not waste our spiritual and physical effort seeking physical gratification, which can never bring us what we truly want and need.

Regardless of our actions during the first eight days, the ninth day of *Yesod* is directly connected to *Malchut*. All that *Malchut* has comes through the channel called *Yesod*, and it is here that we reach the level of physical reality. This is where we invest the most effort in order to form the connection with *Binah*. We must strive to change our desire not only on the level of spiritual thought, as we have done on the first eight days, but also from the foundation. Toward this goal, the kabbalists in general—and The Ari in particular—have supplied us with tools with which to cancel the negative thought consciousness that drives the desire to receive for the self alone.

The act of confession is one of these tools. But to whom do we confess? And why do we confess? Why is it not enough to apologize and express sorrow for what we have done? It seems that there is a certain behavioral pattern specific to Yom Kippur—a kind of special procedure, of which confession is a fundamentally important part. Why is this so?

When we encounter people who have behaved improperly, we demand that they acknowledge their mistakes. When this takes place, we are usually satisfied. The Aramaic word for confession (*vidui*) is connected to certainty and truth, a connection that reveals the true meaning of this act. It does not matter to whom we confess, and it does not matter if anyone is listening to us confess or if anyone has asked us to do so. Confession is an internal matter. It can even be very close to silent. It is well known that The Ari never raised his voice in prayer, a practice we try to emulate. In fact, The Ari was almost completely silent, and only his lips moved during his prayer.

Through confession, we connect to something contrary to the desire to receive for ourselves alone—something contrary to the ego, which claims we are always right, and which will always resist confession. The ego is connected to the physical reality, to the World of Illusion, and therefore cannot tolerate anything that is connected to the World of Truth. Confession enables us to realize the connection to *Binah* so that we may be assured of a year of prosperity and peace. Our goal is a year with no surprises, because surprises are part of the World of Illusion, and they cannot affect us in the World of Truth.

If a person is unwilling to confess, he is holding on to the illusory physical reality of here and now. He cannot go back in time and connect to *Binah*, for it is impossible to be in both worlds—on both levels of consciousness—simultaneously. On all other days of the year, we can act in *Malchut* and at the same time be connected in consciousness to the World of Truth. But we cannot simultaneously hold on both to the consciousness of illusion and to the consciousness of truth. During the year we must be in *Malchut*, but that does not mean we must live in *Malchut*. We do not have to limit our consciousness to the realm of the illusory.

One can exist in *Malchut*, but there is no obligation to live in it. One can escape from it as one would from a prison, for *Malchut* is indeed a kind of prison—an institution that houses the ego and all other illusory attributes. We confess not because we will be well behaved from now on, but because God demands this of us. Confession is a spiritual means of solving problems. Confession offers us an opportunity to escape the grip of *Malchut* and to arrive directly at *Binah*. Confession is the instrument through which we leave the World of Illusion.

The Technology of Fasting

We will now proceed to the issue of the fast, another vital instrument in achieving connection with *Binah*. In *Gate of Meditations*, The Ari quotes Deuteronomy 8:3: "Man does not live by bread only, but by every thing that proceeds out of the mouth of Hashem does he." This verse is actually discussing the difference between the World of Illusion and the World of Truth—between the physical bread that man eats and the non-physical breath that comes from God.

Through the acts of eating and drinking, accompanied by blessings both before and after, we draw blessing into our lives. Food has both physical and spiritual aspects, and a blessing is a channel of communication to the inner aspects. The verse "Man does not live on bread alone" teaches us that we cannot be nourished only by the physical aspect of food. Rather, the internal quality accounts for more than 99% of the food. It is true that without the physical aspect of food, we would have no way to nourish our bodies—but the essence of food's energy lies in its internal quality.

We connect to a food's internal essence through the spiritual channels of communication supplied to us by the Sages, and these channels are called blessings. Yet we are not saying "thank you" to the Creator, because He does not need our thanks, and we are in no way obligated to thank Him. Who asked Him to create food in the first place? Fruit, vegetables, and animals were, after all, created before the creation of the first man. The Creator did not consult with us before He decided to create all of our food sources; He did so as an expression of His inner essence as Creator, to share what He has, whether we are there to receive it or not. Indeed, the moment I accept and enjoy that which the Creator has given, I give the Creator feedback, and with that I close a circle; I am doing my part in bringing wholeness and peace to the universe. Therefore, not only do I have no reason to thank God, but I am actually doing Him a favor by participating in His creative process. By eating, I manifest His thought of sharing and distribution. If I do not pick the fruit and eat it on time, it will drop from the tree and rot. This would then become an act of creation that did not manifest. Blessings can thus be seen not as "thank you's," but rather as cosmic channels of communication.

As mentioned earlier, the connection with *Binah* manifests itself in two aspects, as expressed in Genesis 1 and Genesis 2. Genesis 1 is the creation of the inner reality of the world—the 99%—by *Binah*. Genesis 2 is the creation of the external aspect of the world, or the 1%—which is also accomplished by

Binah. The internal aspect, the heavenly connection, is called *Zeir Anpin*. The external physical reality is called *Malchut*, the earth.

But how is it possible that from *Binah*, the spiritual aspect, came forth the physical earth? Hidden within the physical reality lies an inner thought consciousness called the desire to receive for the self alone. This is *Malchut*. Everything that has a physical nature contains this consciousness. Throughout the year we enjoy the physical aspect. When we consume food and drink while establishing the channels of communication through blessings, we are able to draw abundance only from the external aspect of *Binah*. This is the full extent to which we can communicate with *Binah* during the year. On every other day, only the exterior aspect of *Binah*'s thought consciousness is made available to us.

But this is not the aspect that is realized on *Yom Kippur*. As The Ari said, *Yom Kippur* is our opportunity—for this is the time in which the internal aspect of *Binah* appears. Therefore, when we fast on *Yom Kippur*, we completely cancel the desire to receive for the self alone. And this is the reason for the five restrictions we undertake on *Yom Kippur*. When these restrictions are fulfilled, we succeed in spiritually locking our body's desire to receive; we simply lock it inside, prevent its actual expression, and neutralize it by means of the five restrictions. Only because we have neutralized the desire to receive for the self alone are we able to connect to the internal thought consciousness of *Binah*.

During the year we communicate through blessings, and only through blessings, with the internal qualities of *Binah's* external thought consciousness. This level of *Binah* corresponds in us to the thought consciousness of the desire to receive for the self alone, which is responsible for the activation of the physical body. It is this part of *Binah* that is responsible for the consciousness and force of life that is in food and drink. But even within the body we find internal and external aspects. This distinction exists in everything, in every state of consciousness, and in all *Sfirot*, including *Binah*. Internal and external qualities, Light and Vessel, are present throughout Creation. During the year we act out of *Malchut*, and we therefore connect only with the external qualities of *Binah*. But on *Yom Kippur*, through the five restrictions and neutralization of body consciousness, we are able to connect to the internal qualities of *Binah*—to that consciousness from which we are able to perform surgery on the DNA. This action is not possible using the Vessel of *Binah*, but can be realized only through use of the Light of *Binah*—a Light that is revealed to us only on *Yom Kippur*. And since knowledge is the connection, if we fast and pray on *Yom Kippur* without possessing this knowledge—if it is not clear that the word *vidui* (confession) is connected to the word *vada'ut* (certainty)—then there is no surety that the communication with *Binah* will indeed have been performed. But if we know the purpose of *Yom Kippur's* connections, then we will have the ability to establish with certainty the connection with *Binah*—Light and Vessel, internal and external qualities as one—as required for the performance of DNA surgery.

The moment we rise above body consciousness, however, we are no longer nourished by the external aspect of *Binah*, but rather by its internal qualities. To help us understand the internal essence of *Binah*, The Ari provides us with an example that is as close to its internal qualities as we can imagine. By departing from everything that has even the slightest connection with earthliness, and by understanding the reason for this departure, we can easily connect to the internal qualities of *Binah*.

Prayer, during which we whisper words and exude breath from our mouths, is one of the instruments that brings us closer to the alternate consciousness. This instrument was prepared for us by the Sages. There is no holiday or festival except *Yom Kippur* during which we participate in five prayer services. The five prayer services correspond to the Tree of Life: *Keter*, *Chochmah*, *Binah*, *Zeir Anpin* (which contains *Chesed*, *Gvurah*, *Tiferet*, *Netzach*, *Hod*, and *Yesod*), and *Malchut*. But what is the meaning of the prayers that are said on *Yom Kippur?* The answer is that these prayers are a means of establishing the energy packets—the Sfirot—with which we can create a common bond between our consciousness and the internal qualities of *Binah*. These are the same internal aspects that The Ari described as breath coming out of the mouth.

On the ninth day of the month of Tishrei, on the eve of *Yom Kippur*, we are accustomed to eating in quantity, and in doing so we connect to the fast of *Yom Kippur*, the tenth day of the month. The connection between these two days is extremely close, because kabbalistically it is based on the connection between *Yesod* and *Malchut*, the two Sfirot that embody all substance in the universe. *Malchut* is nourished by *Yesod*, since it has no life of its own. The ninth day is, as stated, connected to the ninth *Sfirah*, *Yesod*, while the tenth day is connected to *Malchut*. As was discussed earlier, it is generally impossible to achieve an internal quality—a kind of Light, like the soul—without an external quality or vessel, such as the physical body. Since on *Yom Kippur Malchut* connects directly to the internal aspect of *Binah* consciousness, the following question arises: Where will *Malchut* receive the external aspect it requires in order to manifest its internal aspect? The answer is revealed to us by the *Talmud* in *Tractate Berachot*, which says that it is essential that on the ninth day we eat double our usual portion, with the explicit intention that the additional food we eat the day before *Yom Kippur* will establish the external thought consciousness of *Malchut*. This is the instrument through which the internal aspect of *Binah* is revealed in the world of *Malchut*.

But how is it possible to establish something in *Malchut* while we are still only on the ninth day, within the domain of the *Sfirah* of *Yesod*? It is possible, despite the fact that *Malchut* is connected to the next day—for *Yesod* and *Malchut* are closely connected to each other. We are unable to make this connection between any other Sfirot, each of which maintains its own independence. Yet another factor that enables the construction of *Malchut's* instrument on the ninth day lies in the intention and consciousness we inject into the food we eat during the meals. Since we intend for the food to establish the external thought consciousness of *Malchut*, this is precisely what happens. It is obvious that without knowledge and understanding, this action cannot manifest.

We now arrive at the taking of the two he-goats by Aaron, the High Priest. But since we have no Temple today—no sacrifices and no High Priest—how does the description presented in Leviticus relate to our lives? A similar question, of course, might be posed with regard to the cosmic communication on Shabbat, when through prayer we travel through space and time to the Revelation on Mount Sinai.

For the present, I will not discuss all of the detailed meanings of the prayer recitation on Shabbat called *Brich Shmae*, which is taken from *The Zohar* and is written in Aramaic. I will also refrain from elaborating on the matter of one's attitude toward the Torah. Suffice it to say that many worshipers find that the time designated for the reading of the Torah is most appropriate for idle conversations with one's neighbor, or for stepping outside for a breath of fresh air.

What becomes clear from this contemporary "syndrome" is that the weekly Torah reading produces no results. Indeed, most of the portions we read seem to have nothing whatsoever to do with our modern lives. Even precepts such as "thou shalt not murder" seem largely irrelevant, for few of us have the inclination to murder or to steal. And what about all of the precepts that deal with the Tabernacle and The Temple, which have not existed for 2,000 years? What is the point of reading them again? Why trouble us with them on Shabbat? Whoever enjoys the melodic reading is invited to attend every Saturday, but those who seek a more profound meaning in *The Bible* must also raise the question: Why, really, do we read the Torah? Most of

what is written in it has nothing to do with our lives today—or
so we assume.

The Zohar says that by reciting the Brich Shmae, we create
a kind of vehicle through which it is possible to perform travel
through time and space, directly to the Revelation on Mount
Sinai. This, then, is our opportunity to connect to the immense
power revealed at that event, in which the first two commandments were given from the mouth of God Himself. Connecting
to this force without knowing what is behind it, however, will
make it difficult for us to get through the week in peace. The
Sages, in their infinite wisdom, decided to integrate Brich
Shmae into the Siddur before removing the Torah from the Ark
because they were familiar with the power embodied in *The
Zohar*. We are like the raiders of the lost Ark, which in fact, for
us, is not lost at all. The Ark, which was located in the Holy of
Holies, was a magnet that attracted the power of tranquillity to
the world, for all mankind and for all life forms on earth. This
lasted until man, in his usual fashion, destroyed the environment. The Ark brought to the world a pure energy of life that
sustained the entire universe. This is the energy to which we
connect on Shabbat. In order for us to connect to this energy,
we must return to Mount Sinai—and according to Rav Shimon
in *The Zohar*, this is possible only with the time machine called
Brich Shmae.

The seemingly unrelated content of the weekly Torah
portions still remains a problem. *The Zohar* goes on to explain
this issue as well. Our existence in the universe has two aspects:

our personal domains, which include everything within each of us, and our surrounding Light—the strong external influence that radiates into each of our personal domains. But what happens to negative thought consciousness on each Shabbat as we stand at the foot of Mount Sinai and connect to the immense power revealed there? What about all the criminals wandering about outside, each of their actions contaminating the universe with negativity? Aren't we all a part of that same universe? How can one protect oneself and not be affected by their actions? In many cases we find ourselves doing things against our own will only as a result of the negative actions of others. How can we protect ourselves from this phenomenon?

The Zohar says that by reading the Torah—by connecting to the energy embodied by Mitzvot such as "thou shall not murder"—we create a protective shield around ourselves. "Thou shall not steal," when declared at the foot of Mount Sinai, creates a protective shield, but only around those who do not steal. Each Shabbat, when we read the mystical cosmic code within the Torah—including all the prohibitions and Mitzvot mentioned in the weekly portions—it helps us personally achieve two goals. The 248 positive commandments are communication channels for attracting positive energy: a force of healing, success, and peace. A Mitzvah is not a command, but rather a means of being together with the Light. There is no commandment to fulfill a Mitzvah, just as there is no command to go see a movie. If the movie is good and enjoyable, we go; if not, we do not go see it. In a similar manner, we choose to eat certain foods because we enjoy them and refrain from others because we do not. The Mitzvot were intended for those who feel a shortage of life energy and wish to replenish that shortage by connecting to the crude positive energy of the universe—the energy revealed at Mount Sinai. On Shabbat, when we read about the Mitzvot that are related to The Temple, we connect through these channels to various aspects of the cosmic energy, regardless of the fact that The Temple is not active at this time. This may perhaps seem strange, but it is part of the perfect cosmic code described by the Torah. It is not possible to cut the Torah up and omit parts of it that do not please us, just as it is not possible to cancel part of the laws of physics under the pretext that we do not like them. If some part of the cosmic code referred to as the Torah has any value at all, then the entire Torah has value. If the Torah contains worthless parts, then it is possible that the entire Torah is worthless.

The Torah is a powerful channel of communication, and one that is highly useful to those who are aware of its power. That is why the phenomenon of an energy shortage is so commonplace, as are environmental problems. Acid rain, rainforest depletion, air and water pollution, the increased mortality rate of freshwater fish—all are the result of an environment that is being purged of the life energy it once had within it. This depletion was brought about by the human desire to receive for oneself, man's negative thought. Man has depleted the universe's energy, and therefore people today feel a shortage of that energy. People cannot imagine the possibility of enjoying themselves seven days a week, and some are even willing to make do with just one moment of happiness in an entire year. Therefore, on

Shabbat, when we read the portion of the week from a kosher Torah scroll, we feed ourselves with the energy that we need for that week as a whole.

If a spiritually unfit and imperfect scroll is used, there is no possibility either of drawing energy to ourselves or of sending energy out into the universe. Kosher Torah scrolls may well be rare just because there are so few people who have the desire and knowledge to connect to the Light through the Torah reading. But we now live in the Age of Aquarius—an age in which people appreciate knowledge. And that is why we at The Kabbalah Centre use only kosher Torah scrolls, by means of which we succeed in connecting to the cosmic energy.

The Mitzvot of reading from the Torah stem from the relationship between the weekly portion and our lives. The weekly portion discusses all the cosmic events that are expected to occur in the course of the coming week. By reading the weekly portion, we ensure that during the entire week, we will act on an alternate level of consciousness without being affected by environmental or social events that we have no ability to prevent. In this way we secure ourselves, week after week, throughout the entire year. Each Shabbat, we are given another opportunity to correct the script expected for the coming week—a script according to which we are affected by the events that take place in the universe around us. But perhaps we may ask, "If I do not steal or murder, if I perform and fulfill the commandments, then why must I read these parts of the Torah again and again, year after year?" The answer is that in order to construct a defense system based on the quantum principle, we must work with the original biblical code.

While one man tries to maintain his moral integrity, another is occupied in negative activities and injecting negativity into the universe. How is it possible to avoid being influenced by this? Though we may not be responsible for environmental pollution, we are indeed affected by it. We are the environment's scapegoat; the mistakes and crimes of others are projected onto us. Although we may manage our lives flawlessly, we nonetheless bear the consequences of others' actions. And we have no way to escape this except by means of the protective wall built around us by the consciousness achieved through the reading of the Torah on Shabbat. This is the purpose of reading from the Torah.

We create this protective wall when we read the Ten Utterances, even when we encounter Mitzvot that appear to be insignificant. Every time we read of various prohibitions related solely to The Temple, which deal through ritual with uncleanness and other issues that are seemingly unrelated to our lives, we form a protective wall that prevents Satan and those who were sent by him—all of whom are expressions of the negativity created by others—from being able to penetrate our lives and hurt us. Reading the Torah on Shabbat protects us from these harmful effects. But what is the connection between all of this and *Yom Kippur*? All of the above is nothing but an introduction—a clarification of the he-goat, also known as the cosmic scapegoat.

As we have said, reading the Torah on *Yom Kippur* enables us to connect to the immense power of *Binah* and to build our own individual protective wall—which in the days of The Temple, when Israelites knew only one way of thought, the positive way—was constructed for the entire universe in a collective fashion. When hatred for no reason took root amongst the Israelites, The Temple ceased to function; the cosmic defense system stopped working, and the reciprocal influence effect began. This effect is what causes us to suffer from the mistakes of others and makes life appear to occur in a seemingly random fashion. As is written in *The Zohar*, Rav Shimon once told his pupils not to leave the house, for on that day—as was the case at the time of the Plague of the First-born, on the night of the Exodus from Egypt—the Angel of Death was granted permission to kill anyone he might encounter. Rav Shimon was the personification of *Binah* on earth. Therefore, he knew about expected events and was able to warn his pupils accordingly. Rav Shimon knew everything that happened or was about to take place at all ends of the universe, beyond the bounds of time, space, and motion. He thus saw the Angel of Death descending. On any other day, Rav Shimon could forbid the Angel of Death to act and command him to return to the Upper World just as quickly as he came—but not on this day. He therefore warned his pupils not to leave the house.

A Deeper Look at Yom Kippur

The word kippur is spelled, in its standard spelling, כ פ ו ר (*Caf-Pei-Vav-Resh*). These four letters form the two combinations כ ו (*Caf Vav*) and פ ר (*Pei Resh*). *Caf Vav* equals 26, which is the numerical value of the Tetragrammaton. The Ari notes in *Gate of Meditations* that the word Kippur includes the encryption of *Caf Vav*—the encoded message that we will use in order to successfully complete our mission to remove Satan consciousness from our lives. In fact, the holiday is called *Yom Kippur* and appears in the plural form in the Torah. This pluralization hints at the existence of two levels of awareness that serve to complete the execution of the task. The conscious level, and the link to the outer space, is the *Caf Vav*, which connects us to *Binah*.

We refer to *Yom Kippur* as *Binah*. But what is the meaning of *Binah*? It is consciousness. Without going into too much detail, it can be said that *Binah* is the place where nothing is illusory. This is because illusion belongs solely to the realm of the mind and physical senses, the realm of *Malchut*. *Binah* and *Malchut* are two complementary aspects of the desire to receive, and they must thus be integrated. But there is one basic difference between them: *Malchut* contains the Tree of Knowledge of Good and Evil. When we say that a certain person has attained *Binah* consciousness, we are therefore speaking of a person who knows not a trace of evil—a person who is connected to the Tree of Life, who is all *Chesed*, or, as The Ari says, who loves to do good. This is *Binah* consciousness. And it is called *Yom Kippur* because on this day we must integrate the two aspects of the desire to receive. To be sure, there is nothing wrong with the actual desire to receive. But when it includes the desire to receive for the self alone, then it is *Malchut* consciousness—the consciousness in which most human beings are, unfortunately, to be found. This is the consciousness in which people say, "But this is the real world." Yet what kind of real world is it that contains only chaos, misfortune, and disease? Is there a real world in which all of this does not exist? If there exists a man who lives in such a world, then he can only be a spiritual man who is not involved in hatred.

The generation in which The Temple was destroyed was a generation of hatred for no reason. Any person who is involved in hatred brings ruin and disorder unto the universe. Good people are connected to *Binah* consciousness, like Aaron the High Priest, who was all *Chesed*. The Torah does not tell us that there once lived a priest named Aaron, and that he was a channel for *Binah* consciousness. Why was he a channel for *Binah* consciousness? Because he loved *Chesed*. In my book

Power of Aleph Beth, it is written that Aaron was chosen for his role because he was always busy making peace between people. He did not deal with hatred, not even when it was justified—for hatred does not enable the attaining of *Binah* consciousness. Without *Binah* consciousness, one can sit in synagogue and pray forever, but it would all be for naught. There is no chance of removing the Satan consciousness from one's life as long as there remains within us even an inkling of hatred of any kind.

It seems that what results from the message encrypted in *Yom Kippur* is that we have an addition to *Malchut*, which is the physical world. On the tenth day of the month of Tishrei, we are affected by a phenomenon called *Binah*. Of all the days of the year, it is on this day only that an external intelligence visits our world, *Zeir Anpin* and *Malchut*, the seven lower Sfirot from which our world is composed. This external intelligence is called *Binah*. Yet while this visit is indeed from another world, it is a world that is located not somewhere in outer space but rather here and now, within and around us. Scientists were disappointed to discover that there are no green creatures with antennae on Mars. If so, where are those creatures that live outside of planet earth? Where are they hiding? They are not hiding at all. Although *Binah* exists and is present among us, it remains concealed from our eyes in order to enable us to remove Bread of Shame.

Unfortunately, when the Torah provided us with the event called *Yom Kippur* and specified the tenth day of the month of Tishrei as the most sacred day of the year, a misleading aspect of religiosity was immediately introduced. That day came to be regarded as "a day filled with religious admiration," or a day on which we are supposed to feel such religious admiration that the concept of confession is added to our prayers—a concept that does not exist on any other day of the year. This perception is misleading, and it is one that distracts worshipers' consciousness from the issue at hand.

On *Yom Kippur*, *Binah* and *Malchut* join forces; the Upper and Lower kingdoms unite into a single entity. And when you connect to such a wonderful and harmonious entity—to such a remote consciousness—the entire world is in your hand. That is why the Torah employs the plural form of Yom Kippurim and not *Yom Kippur*; it is to inform us that both aspects (embodied in the Aramaic letter ה (*Hei*), which appears twice in the יהוה (*Yud Hei Vav Hei*)) are combined on this day. As mentioned, the letter *Yud* corresponds with Chochmah; the first *Hei* with *Binah*; *Vav* with *Zeir Anpin*, the connection with outer space; and the final *Hei* with *Malchut*. This is the potential state of the great unification of *Binah* and *Malchut*—and the manifestation of the unification depends on each and every person's connection with the potential state of consciousness, the unification of *Binah* and *Malchut*. Yet this is not immediately available to us. One cannot simply say, "I am going to meditate; I am going to connect." Instead, there are many laws and preliminary conditions that must first be fulfilled. Many channels of communication must be established through which we can later realize the connection with *Binah*.

On *Yom Kippur*, *Binah* comes out from behind the curtain, climbs up on stage, and appears before us in a way that enables us to connect to it. But if we do not even know what we want to connect to, it will not matter how much we pray, how much we confess, and to what degree we abide by all other principles. If we do not know to what, where, or why we connect, our prayer will be all but useless. To be sure, this does not mean that one should not go to the synagogue, or not do that which our inner voice pleads with us to do. All that is needed in order to realize the connection is simply to know, and the knowledge will enable the manifestation of the connection.

As mentioned earlier, for ten days we try to purify ourselves, to destroy the embodiment of the negative consciousness over which we are responsible. This process involves ten sections of Satan's realm. Each day requires us to remove another aspect of Satan, according to the Ten Sfirot—one *Sfirah* on each day. We start with *Keter*, on the first of Tishrei. After that, on the second day of *Rosh Hashanah*, we purify ourselves and then attack and destroy Satan's *Sfirah* of Chochmah. Then, on the third day, we deal with *Binah*—and so on until the tenth day, on which we reach *Malchut*. If on this day we succeed in realizing the mission of attacking and destroying Satan, we can then connect to *Binah*.

Only on the tenth day—only on the tenth *Sfirah*—can the final attack and destruction of the embodiment of the negative energy called *Malchut* take place. On the tenth day we have reached the level of purification of *Malchut*, the desire to receive, which has become the desire to receive in order to share. This degree of purity is attained through various stages during the Ten Days of Repentance, which are equal to each other in importance. Primarily on the eve of *Yom Kippur*, which is secondary in importance only to *Yom Kippur* itself, it is especially important to have the correct consciousness in order to communicate with *Binah*. God has appointed *Binah* to assist us in life. For this reason, the Creator arranged the universe in such a way that once a year *Binah*, our lifeline and energy reservoir, leaves its realm—the realm of the highest consciousness—and appears in our realm. The stage is at *Binah's* disposal only on the tenth day of the month of Tishrei. This, then, is the meaning of Tishrei and of *Yom Kippur*, and it deals not merely with a sacred day—a day of admiration, regret, and the rest of the atonement package. This is the day of *Binah*.

All this comes from *The Zohar* and from the writings of The Ari. The writings of The Ari, which interpret and explain *The Zohar*, were disseminated and have been available to the public since long before the writing of this book. If anyone has any complaints, they should therefore address them to The Ari and to his close followers, Rav Chaim Vital and his son, Rav Shmuel, who put it all into writing so as to impart it unto future generations. These words were written and disseminated without restriction, although a danger always existed that they might fall into the wrong hands. Yet Rav Isaac Luria declared that this knowledge is not dangerous to anybody. We are in the Age of Aquarius, and there is no turning back. The average man on the street is capable of this communication. It is important to understand that *Yom Kippur* is not a collection of Mitzvot and restrictions that we carry out; it is the day on which *Binah* is revealed on Earth. All of our actions in the synagogue on this day are nothing but a result of this cosmic event—the appearance of *Binah*, the consciousness that is so crucial to the spiritual well-being and physical existence of every person in the world. This is the meaning and significance of *Yom Kippur*. Anything else surrounding *Yom Kippur* is secondary.

Genesis 1:1 reads, "In the beginning God created the heaven and the earth." Of course, this heaven and earth are not the heaven and earth we know but rather the seven Sfirot, those packets of energy or seven qualities of consciousness—*Chesed, Gvurah, Tiferet, Netzach, Hod, Yesod*, and *Malchut*. And for that, seven days of Creation were required. Who created this phenomenon? Who created the beginning of the spiritual negative consciousness, with which the seven days of Creation deal?

In the seven days of Creation described in Genesis 1, nothing physical was created, only consciousness—seven levels of thought consciousness and nothing more. Who created these levels of consciousness before they were realized in a spiritual manner as described in Genesis 1, and before they were expressed in a physical manner as described in Genesis 2? The answer is *Binah*. *The Zohar* states that the word *barah* (created) explains this, for bri'ah (creation) is connected to *Binah*. *The Zohar* therefore reveals to us the secret of *Binah*. The cosmic *Binah* is the source of all reasons in the world. It is the origin of the seven Sfirot. It is hard to believe that this consciousness of *Binah* is what led to the realization of all the galaxies in the universe and, of course, to the realization of our earth as well. This source, which existed before the first moment of Creation, is revealed to us now. Why? So that we may connect directly to the source of the essence of Creation.

This might be likened to a physician who tries as hard as he can to reach the fetus long before the birth process in order to determine if it has any defects. The physician aspires to connect to the fetus, to examine and investigate it, and if necessary to give it the required treatment—even surgery—at its most fundamental level. Such is the purpose of *Yom Kippur*: not to create another holiday or to burden us with an additional load, but to assist us in performing surgery on our own individual cassettes, which are defined according to our previous reincarnations. If we are able to connect to the original source, to the creation of all creations, we will be able to become the surgeons of our cassettes and thereby remove from them the superfluous sections—sections that might introduce disorder, trouble, disease, and disruption into our lives.

If you choose life, and if in your opinion everything around seems hopeless and helpless, you may be sure that from a kabbalistic standpoint there is indeed much to be done. Yet there is hope. There is one day a year called *Yom Kippur* through which we have the ability to connect—to sit together with *Binah* on the throne, and to consult with it as to the correction and, if necessary, the improvement of our existence in the coming year. We are actually returning in order to correct our future. But all of this is possible only after we have completely destroyed the desire to receive for the self alone, which is embodied through Satan.

Strange as it may seem, *The Zohar* and the writings of The Ari explicitly reveal that we have the ability to change reality. The Ari raises the following question: After a person, God forbid, loses an arm or a leg or any other part of his physical body, why does he not grow back the missing limb? The Ari claims that in the Age of Aquarius, the knowledge that causes man's genetic code to reconstruct the missing organ—as he first did when the fetus developed during the pregnancy—will once more be discovered. This is knowledge that has been lost since the time of Rav Shimon Bar Yochai. The Ari further predicts that in the Age of Aquarius, many changes will take place in the way we regard the universe around us. And when we all undergo spiritual rebirth, it is evident that we will also undergo physical rebirth. What came first, the chicken or the egg? There is no need to go back to that lesson again. Everyone knows the answer; The spiritual entity, the concept, the thought will always precede the revelation and physical expression. "The end of action starts in thought," said the Kabbalist Rav Shlomo Alkabetz from Safed, the author of the song "Lecha Dodi." The primary thought underlies any physical event. This is the gift given to us on *Yom Kippur*—not religiosity, but an opportunity to increase and improve the spiritual and physical quality of life of all human beings.

With this understanding of *Yom Kippur*, we may now proceed toward an understanding of the manner in which we connect to *Binah*. This is what *Binah* offers us on this important day—and now it is obvious why it is important and holy. Holy means whole, complete, perfect, and balanced. A circle, as opposed to a line, expresses a perfect connection and the absence of limitations. *The Zohar* says that on this day, we have the ability to change any physical impediment that is likely to appear in our personal lives during the coming year. And if our cassettes contain defects, interruptions, despair, or sorrow, then we have the chance, once a year, to change all that with the aid of *Binah*.

With the meaning of *Yom Kippur* clear to us, we may take the opportunity and use the power of *Binah*. But there is one prerequisite: God's promise that Satan's army will never be able to use the information we have about *Rosh Hashanah* and *Yom Kippur*. Our attack-and-destroy mission is aimed at Satan's army, against the troops of the Death Star, who aspire to wreak havoc, destruction, and death among all human beings. The action of this army and, unfortunately, its power as well, are realized through acts against humanity. Yet if we are concerned that the Death Star troops might make use of this information, we may rest assured that *Yom Kippur* has a secret—a structured safety valve—that will prevent them from doing so. There is a most basic translation of the name *Yom Kippur*, a day that is like Purim. The Talmud and *The Zohar* state that toward the end of the Age of Aquarius, after peace rules the earth, only one holiday will remain, only a single cosmic event—Purim, which is celebrated in the month of Adar, under the sign of Pisces. Why this holiday only? Is the Torah not eternal? Actually, it is not. The body of the Torah is not eternal; it is part of linear time. It came into existence 2,000 years before the creation of the world in order to elevate the human species from a linear, cyclical, and finite existence to an eternal existence of unity. Purim is the first holiday on which unity between human beings was evident, the realization of "love your neighbor as yourself." But perhaps one might ask, If we were successful on Purim in realizing the almost impossible task of fulfilling "love your neighbor as yourself," why did the Persian people not bring about the Age of Aquarius?

The answer is that not all souls were present in the world at that time. During the Revelation at Mount Sinai, everyone was present, but not all souls that participated in the Sin of the Golden Calf were present at Purim to rectify their sin. At the Sin of the Golden Calf, the desire to receive for the self alone reared its ugly head. On the festival of Purim, the ugly head otherwise known as Satan expired—but it expired only to the extent that all souls were enabled to reincarnate in order to appear again. After that we continued to ruin that vision of perfection, and we continue to do so to this very day. In any case, the secret code of *Yom Kippur*, which explains how to achieve the cosmic connection with *Binah* consciousness, depends entirely on the fulfillment of "love your neighbor as yourself."

This brings us to another issue. Is there any similarity between Tish'ah Be'av and *Yom Kippur*? On both days we fulfill the five restrictions, although for different reasons. On the ninth day of *Av*, *Binah* is not revealed. As the Torah tells us, only on *Yom Kippur* does the potential internal aspect of *Binah* appear, and all that is needed in order to reveal it lies in the actions taken on this day and on the nine preceding days.

One of the most important restrictions performed on *Yom Kippur* is the fast. In his volume entitled Gate of the Holy Spirit, The Ari discusses healing meditations for every ailment imaginable. In this volume, he also identifies a single common denominator to all healing meditations: fasting. The body's primary and only inclination is that of the desire to receive, and there is no greater neutralization of this property than fasting. Kabbalistically, the only reason disease occurs lies in the manifestation of the desire to receive for the self alone. Therefore, the neutralization of ego desire removes the source of the disease and initiates the therapeutic process. Total neutralization of the desire to receive completely precludes any possibility of disease.

But fasting alone is not enough; meditation is required as well. In Gate of the Holy Spirit, The Ari says that this process, which has been kept secret since the days of Rav Shimon Bar Yochai, will be revealed in the Age of Aquarius to all of mankind.

The Ari explains that throughout the year, one cannot live on physical bread alone. To the contrary, it is also necessary to connect to the internal aspect of the food, to the words of God. The cosmic code embodied in the Torah teaches us that without awareness of the internal aspect called *hevel* (breath), we are limited to partaking of physical food alone. This concept has been understood by members of all religions who raise their voices in prayer before breaking bread. Such prayer should, however, contain a connection to the inner force located within the bread. What "man cannot live on bread alone" really means is that man cannot ensure protection to his close environment unless he extracts the inner consciousness from within that bread and integrates it into his existence using the appropriate blessing. All this takes place, as stated, year round. But on *Yom Kippur*, a different procedure of communication is followed. On *Yom Kippur* we communicate with the internal aspect of *Binah*, which prepares us for the DNA surgery.

Let us now return to the question that was raised earlier with regard to the he-goats in Leviticus 16:7-8:

"And he shall take the two goats, and set them before Hashem at the door of the Tent of Meeting. And Aaron shall cast lots upon the two goats: one lot for Hashem, and the other lot for Azazel." Here again, the subject of slaughtering and sacrificing animals seems inhumane to many of us, embodying as it does an expression of cruelty to animals. Nevertheless, while the biblical code explicitly denounces cruelty to animals, the same code reveals that there are animals that have come into this world specifically to be sacrificed. This is the way in which they can share and bring abundance to the world, advance in the *tikkun* (correction) process, and accomplish their purpose of creation. For this reason, we should not prevent them from doing so.

Just as the same action can be a blessing to one and a curse to another, what seems cruel to one can signify *tikkun* to another. We have neither the ability nor the right to determine what is suitable for the animal and what is not. To be sure, the causing of suffering is strictly prohibited under any circumstance. In fact, the ceremonious ritual slaughter according to the laws of Kashrut is performed using a sharp and absolutely smooth knife, which passes over the windpipe and main artery leading to the brain. According to the Talmud, an animal that is slaughtered in this manner feels as if a gust of wind has blown across its face and brought it to rest in peace. On the other hand, if someone shoots an animal to death or kills it in any other manner, it is prohibited, just as is murder.

I am not calling for immediate suspension of all hunting permits issued throughout the world, but wish only to note that the Torah completely prohibits any cruelty toward animals. But who can determine, from a quantum perspective, that which is good and evil? As long as an animal does not suffer, who is authorized to stand up and claim that it is bad for the animal and contrary to its best interests? I agree that no animal's life should be taken unless, in its death, that animal has revealed an aspect of sharing. It may therefore be said that in general, the sacrifices mentioned in the biblical code are not intended to please God, who has no need for them at all, but rather for the purpose of *tikkun*.

The only difference between man and animal lies in the intensity of the desire to receive. The animal has a lower IQ than man not because its intelligence is less, but because its desire to receive for itself is not as strong as that exhibited by the human race. Human beings enjoy the privilege and the responsibility of sacrificing themselves, and sacrifice is not always measured in terms of relinquishing life. To the contrary, there are many ways in which to sacrifice. As long as the animals are not slaughtered in vain and do not experience suffering, and as long as that slaughtering takes place according to the timing and instructions encoded in the Torah, then on that specific day they are filled with joy—for they have then achieved the completion of their personal *tikkun*.

It is true that by giving milk animals have an opportunity to share as well, but through sacrifice they can share with the entire universe at the highest level. The Torah clarifies this point when it mentions sacrifices. Animals also have destiny, according to which they can serve as channels for Light that can improve the quality of the universe—an improvement that will benefit all fruit and vegetables as well as all existing animals in every kingdom, including our own. Man has continuously polluted the world for many years, and it is therefore necessary to join in the effort to improve the quality of the universe. Positive human activity is one way to do so. Connecting to *Binah* consciousness is another. For what we strive to achieve for ourselves is certainly not meant for ourselves alone, but is simply a step on the way to helping the greater whole. Correction of the genetic code on our personal cassettes is a condition we require in order to help improve the quality of life of others. I can share with others only that which I already have, like the Talmud and the Kabbalah. And if I experience peace and fulfillment—if I experience happiness—I can share it with others. But if I am filled with pain, sorrow, despair, anxiety, and grief, I can share these as well. Unfortunately, the vast majority of people are all too willing to share their negative qualities with their environment.

Let us now recall the question regarding the relationship between the he-goat, the actions of the High Priest in The Temple, and our lives here and now. We have no Temple, but does that mean we are not able to reach the reservoir of energy called *Binah* and perform this communication? The Torah explains essentially all of its various aspects: laying the hands of the High Priest on the goat's head, casting the lots, and sending one of the goats out into the desert in the hands of an appointed man. If these Mitzvot are impossible to perform properly in this day and age, how can we connect with *Binah*? Why even bother to consider it?

The answer has already been given: In the days of The Temple, none of us had to be concerned with the quantum, for the High Priest, through The Temple, dealt with it for us. The Temple was constantly connected to *Binah* and attracted energy to the universe—energy that wrapped and protected us at all times from the evil created by all those who stole, murdered, or even conceived of a negative thought anywhere on the face of the earth. The Temple was situated in Jerusalem because therein lies the energy center of the universe. The Holy of Holies on The Temple Mount in Jerusalem is where the corrected *Malchut*—the desire to receive in order to share—is revealed in its most concentrated and powerful form. The Holy of Holies means the whole of all wholes—the most harmonious of all that is harmonious.

This is where the desire to receive for the sake of sharing completely connected with the Light force of the Creator on the quantum level. The Temple prevented uncontrolled outbursts of energy throughout the universe, but not only on the face of the earth; harmony prevailed over all planets. No supernovas erupted, as they do today. Harmony reigned in the vegetable, animate, and inanimate kingdoms as well. The air was clean, the water was pure, and pollution did not plague the environment. The process of destruction and erosion did not take place in the world while The Temple existed.

But what can we do today, without The Temple, to defend ourselves against the negative energy that is polluting the universe? How can we protect the spiritual genetic code, which includes both the physical DNA and all of our environmental conditions? Are we destined to suffer like the fish that swim in polluted waters? Are we destined to breathe polluted air? Are we destined to live in a disharmonious social and familial environment, which is also a result of the pollution and destruction of the environment? How will we be saved from the earthquakes, floods, or storms that are all a result of the negativity injected by man into the universe? How will we defend ourselves? How will we take all of the negative energy we have created and cast it on the scapegoat so that it will take all universal negativity upon itself and leave us and our environment in a state of perfect energetic cleanliness? Is it within our power to erect a protective wall to purify not only the air we breathe and the water we drink, but also the entire universe in which we live, including all galaxies? Is it within our power to promise a cassette that contains a life completely unscathed by all the negativity around us?

The reply to all these questions is affirmative. We have previously learned from *The Zohar* that reading the Torah allows for the establishment of just such a protective wall each week. Now, in the context of *Yom Kippur*, we will make use of this knowledge.

The quantum effect is responsible for the perfect order that reigns in our world—a world in which a cause precedes every effect. However, those who do not identify the causes may get the impression that the effects are nothing more than a random series of events. To the contrary, nothing is arbitrary in our world. The only thing that seemingly creates an effect of coincidence is the negative activity of human beings. Hatred is embodied and expressed in a way that appears to be random. The negative energy postpones the revelation of the Light force of the Creator in the world. This system gives man the opportunity to remove Bread of Shame. It seems The Temple is not here for us today, and so the protective wall that it provided does not cover us. But this description is not precise, for in truth, The Temple exists even today, here and now, as does its power. But The Temple is, as Rav Shimon says, heavily concealed in the physical realm. As a result, it will act and protect only those who know it and can connect to the immense power it attracted to the world at the time it was still visible. Up until 2,000 years ago, The Temple offered protection to all, without exception. Now it offers protection only to those who connect to it, just as we connect to it on *Yom Kippur*. And this connection is the connection to *Binah*.

We live in a free universe—one in which all men have freedom of choice. In the month of Tishrei, Satan and his armada are granted permission to manifest the objective of their existence. We, on the other hand, are granted permission to create the connection with *Binah*. But we have a problem: How do we avoid the negative energy that people have injected into the universe? It will not disappear simply because we ignore it. In order for us to create a global environment of peace and tranquillity, certain activities must be performed and are required of all people in the world. On *Yom Kippur*, we are given the opportunity to find a scapegoat, to cast all of the negative energy we have accumulated in the course of the year onto it, and to let Satan and his armada express their essence in relation to that goat. Satan insists on his right to maintain his presence in the world, and like a dog waiting for a bone, he does not let go until he receives something from us.

Man has injected negativity into the universe, as has been made all too apparent by environmental pollution. Forests around us are dying; pure water is disappearing. There is no longer fresh air for breathing—air that may be breathed free of charge. Kabbalah explains that if something must be paid for, it is a sure sign that it is illusory—for all the good things in life that are connected to the World of Truth are given to us free of charge. Fish do not cost money; anyone can cast his rod and fish. Air does not cost money; anyone can breathe it on his own. People who are busy buying expensive things are dealing with the physical reality, the World of Illusion. But Satan and his entire band do not dwell in the World of Illusion. They know very well what is real and what is not, and they are out hunting for prey. In the month of Tishrei, they demand that their voice be heard, and God has given them this opportunity. So in this month, they will locate their victims. The question that remains is, who will these victims be? This is what *Yom Kippur* is about, and that is why we read about the cosmic scapegoat in the Torah.

But why don't we use scape-candy, or a scape-lion? Why only a scapegoat? And what is the meaning of the word Azazel? Is the Torah so powerful that we do not have the ability to understand the terms it uses? The Torah itself remains concealed and confidential, like a root buried underground. According to Leviticus 16:10, "But the goat, on which the lot fell for Azazel, shall be set alive before Hashem, to make atonement over him, to send him away for Azazel into the wilderness." The goat was released into the desert at a place called Azazel. And how did the goat collect from throughout the universe and take upon itself all of the negative energy created by all mankind in the course of an entire year? All this on the small head of one goat? How is it possible? How can people be so naïve as to believe in such things?

In order to protect the entire universe, a High Priest is needed. But how was the Priest, or Kohen, chosen? In Numbers 16, Korach complains to Moses about the way in which he was appointed High Priest. Korach rebelled, and what happened? He succeeded in inciting the entire camp to rise up against Moses. But after the earth opened its mouth and swallowed him and all of his company, the Israelite People remained bewildered, divided, and dejected. This situation brought upon the Israelites the tragedy of the Sin of the Spies, a tragedy whose results were discernible for many years to come. Contrary to Korach's opinion, it seems that not anyone could become a Kohen, a Priest—and certainly not a High Priest.

What is special about Aaron the Priest? This is what Korach did not understand. Aaron was not chosen by a human being; it was not Moses who appointed Aaron, but rather the Creator. Aaron was the personification of *Chesed*, the embodiment of giving and caring for one's fellow men. He was therefore suited to serve as High Priest—to transfer all human sins unto the goat's head and to build, in this way, a perfect shield with which to protect the inhabitants of the entire world from trouble and misfortune for the entire year.

The inner essence of the scapegoat issue is that we can draw blessing from the well for us all, even though the stone upon the well's mouth is large. The large stone represents Satan and his band. They are standing at the mouth of the well in order to feed off of it and prevent people from enjoying the fruits of God's blessings. How are they defeated? In Psalms 23:5, it is written, "You prepared a table before me in the presence of my enemies."

Rav Shimon offers us answers to many of the questions we have raised regarding scapegoats and other related issues. He explains that the reason Joseph chose to imprison Shimon, of all people, is that Shimon and Levi always opened the door for judgment. That is what happened with Joseph, and it is also what happened in Shechem, when the two brothers slew all men in the city with absolute judgment, with not a bit of mercy.

Rav Shimon therefore warns us not to take the Torah stories literally, but rather to use them as a means of understanding the cosmic code. Moses separated Levi from Shimon and the rest of the brothers so that he would not awaken judgment among the Tribes of Israel. Joseph knew that Shimon, the channel for harsh judgment—together with Levi, the channel for soft judgment—could conquer and destroy the entire world. By imprisoning Shimon, Joseph removed the power of judgment from the world. The tribe of Levi was separated from the other tribes, was not given any land, and was sanctified to serve The Temple—not because there were vacant positions in the Tent of Meeting, but rather because Joseph sought to separate them from Shimon, thereby separating these two kinds of negative consciousness from one another. The story of Shechem does not deal with murder and genocide, but rather demonstrates that when the complete connection between two kinds of negative consciousness is realized, Satan receives unlimited power, bringing total destruction and ruin to the environment and to society. This story illustrates the principle that dictates that when free choice occurs on the spiritual level, a consequence necessarily results on the physical level.

Rav Shimon explains that if we wish to prevent disasters from occurring in life, we must fully activate the spiritual level—to separate and neutralize the two kinds of judgment in advance. If we do not make this effort, their destructive action in the world will be the unavoidable result. Joseph knew this and imprisoned Shimon on a spiritual level. After that, he knew that there was nothing more to fear.

What is **SUKKOT?**

*S*ukkot, like *Yom Kippur*, connects us to the universe's immense power. Unfortunately, like *Yom Kippur*, the meaning of this holiday is widely misunderstood as well. *Sukkot*—also called the Feast of Booths—begins on the 15th day of Tishrei. According to most commentators, this holiday is intended to remind us of the booths (*Sukkot*, the plural of which is *Sukkah*) in which the Israelites resided in the desert following their Exodus from Egypt. The holiday lasts seven days.

The Torah's first mention of *Sukkot* is in Exodus 23, where it is described as the Feast of Harvest and as the last in a sequence of three holidays: *Pesach*, *Shavuot*, and *Sukkot*. *Rosh Hashanah* and *Yom Kippur* are also holidays, of course, but *Pesach*, *Shavuot*, and *Sukkot* are set apart.

Sukkot is a holiday of satisfaction and of resignation. These words, however, should not be interpreted as one would ordinary, mundane emotions; instead, they refer here to spiritual growth and rebirth. After the ten days of *Rosh Hashanah* and *Yom Kippur*, in which we have made decisions to aid us in our transformation, *Sukkot* emerges as a joyous holiday. Despite this, many people neglect *Sukkot*, while many others observe only parts of the holiday. This may be because constructing the *Sukkah* and eating meals within it "far from the comforts of home" entails a certain amount of inconvenience. To many, it seems like a lot of work for commemorating an ancient people's desert habitats.

According to Kabbalah, however, we do not celebrate *Sukkot* or any other holiday just to memorialize something that happened to our ancestors. Rather, *Sukkot* has cosmic importance—a significance that emerges from our understanding of the Torah as a coded document. This code deals with the act of constructing a *Sukkah*, but the cause for the action lies elsewhere.

Did the Israelites really have a choice in the kinds of lodgings they made for themselves in the desert? Could they have rented apartments? If they had no choice, and if they did only what they had to do, why did the Creator bring about another holiday to interrupt the normal conduct of our lives? Are we going to all this trouble just to remind ourselves of the harsh conditions that existed 2,000 years ago? Does this not contradict the Torah, where it is written,

"Therefore choose life"—meaning a life filled with comfort and serenity?

Yet *Sukkot* arrives and requires that we leave our homes for seven days and live in a *Sukkah*. We must therefore investigate the inner meaning of the cosmic code that can explain this practice. Leviticus 23:39 reads: "Howbeit on the fifteenth day of the seventh month, when you have gathered in the fruits of the land, you shall keep the feast of Hashem seven days; on the first day shall be a solemn rest, and on the eighth day shall be a solemn rest."

In other words, since we are in a time of harvest during which our material needs are satisfied, we give our thanks to God in a manner similar to the secular holiday of Thanksgiving. But does God really need our thanks? We read in Deuteronomy: "You shall keep the feast of tabernacles seven days, after that thou hast gathered in from your threshing-floor and from your winepress. And you shall rejoice in your feast, you, and your son, and your daughter . . . "

Here again, it seems that we are to give thanks for the harvest. But our understanding of the Torah as a code tells us that a physical event by itself can never constitute the reason for anything written therein. The meaning of the holiday, therefore, is not a reminder of the harsh conditions in the desert or the bounty of a harvest. Instead, Kabbalah teaches that the holiday connects us to the Creator—that is, to the Godlike elements within ourselves. When this connection has been made, all despair, pain, and suffering associated with the physical realm disappear. Indeed, the Torah tells us to "choose life"—and this choice is not limited to the material level. Once we understand this, we must ask many questions that seem to refer to the physical dimension. The correct answers to those questions will reveal the holiday's truly cosmic significance.

What is the purpose of *Sukkot*? Why does it fall on the 15th day of Tishrei? Where does the name *Sukkah* originate? And why must we reside in one?

A more specific question concerns the roof of the *Sukkah*, which must be made of cut trees and never of metal or of glass. It is written that we must be able to see the stars through the roof. Why is this important? And if the night is cloudy, have we not fulfilled this requirement?

We are also told that that the shadowed area created by the *Sechach* (literally, covering) cannot be greater than the area that is not shadowed by it. What does this refer to?

According to Kabbalah, these questions will direct us to the true reality—the 99% reality. We will even want to ask additional questions in order to receive more answers and forge a stronger connection.

Why does the harvest of the crops take place in Tishrei? It is clear that purely agricultural reasons are insufficient to explain this, so we must look deeper.

Tradition interprets *Sukkot* as a holiday that unifies the sun and the moon, and brings two cycles to harmony and completion. This sounds nice, but what does it mean?

In Leviticus 23:9, the connection between the holiday and the harvest is emphasized. Its mention in Deuteronomy also places an emphasis on the harvest. Is *Sukkot*, therefore, a matter of saying "thank you" to God? And what about the majority of us who are not farmers—must we celebrate as well?

Some say that the *Sukkah* is supposed to bring us joy and a feeling of security. But the truth of the matter is that our own homes give us much more security than the *Sukkah* ever could impart. Moreover, precisely how is the *Sukkah* supposed to bring us joy? We should note that joy is related neither to *Pesach* nor to *Shavuot*. Thus it is written in Deuteronomy 16:15: "Seven days shall you keep a feast unto Hashem your God in the place which He shall choose; because Hashem, your God shall bless you in all thine increase, and in all the work of your hands, and you shall be altogether joyful."

This passage refers only to *Sukkot* and not to the two other holidays. In fact, it is mentioned in the *Amidah* prayer that the only holiday on which we connect with joy is *Sukkot*: "this Festival of *Sukkot*, season of our rejoicing."

But what about all other holidays? Are some holidays entirely without joy? Might there not be people who experience greater joy on *Shavuot* or on *Pesach* than on *Sukkot?*

In Kings I, 8:1-3, it is written:

> Then Solomon assembled the elders of
> Israel, and all the heads of the tribes, the princes
> of the fathers' houses of the children of Israel,
> unto King Solomon in Jerusalem, to bring up
> the Ark of the Covenant of Hashem out of the
> city of David, which is Zion. And all the men of
> Israel assembled themselves unto King Solomon
> at the feast, in the month *Eitanim*, which is the
> seventh month. And all the elders of Israel came,
> and the priests took up the Ark.

King Solomon finished the building of The Temple on
Sukkot. Was this planned? Was the construction fortuitously
completed in the month of *Eitanim? Eitanim* means "forces"
and is thus the month of forces. But what is the significance
of moving the Ark from Zion to Jerusalem? Why did they
not immediately place the Ark in Jerusalem? Why did they
wait? Later, in Chapter 8, Solomon asks: "But will God in
very truth dwell on the earth? Behold, heaven and the heav-
en of heavens cannot contain Thee; how much less this
house that I have built!"

This may seem a strange finish to the construction of
The Temple. Why did Solomon build The Temple in the
first place if he doubted the Creator's ability to be contained
in The Temple?

Without having answers to the questions just posed, we can fall into the trap of blindly following tradition for tradition's sake. But the answer to all of these questions revolves around one simple fact: the Torah was given to us in order to offer us insight into the universe—insight that lies beyond the capabilities of our five senses. In order to connect with the energy that will benefit our lives, we must do what is required of us. In the universe, as in the seasons of the year, different energies are revealed on different days. Only by raising our consciousness can we be begin to understand what is really going on in the inner reality of the 99% realm. Therefore, if the Torah declared the 15th day of Tishrei a holiday, some cosmic event must occur on that day that can benefit us. The cosmic hardware is available on that day, and we must install the software.

Sukkot is connected, according to *The Zohar*, to the left-column consciousness of the Vessel. Does this mean that we are dealing with a negative holiday? Of course not; the left column is based on the precept that "the human heart's inclination is evil from its youth." Man is born with the instinctive desire to receive for the self alone. During the period between *Rosh Hashanah* and *Sukkot*, our objective is to transform that desire into one for the sake of sharing. Our intention here is not to destroy the desire to receive; rather, it is to change the desire to receive so that it operates according to the principle of the right column, the desire to share. Using the Torah's software, we are able to do this on *Sukkot*.

Concerning the actions and Mitzvot to be performed on *Sukkot*, we read in Leviticus 23:40: "And you shall take you on the first day of fruit of goodly trees, branches of palm trees, and boughs of thick trees, and willows of the brook, and you shall rejoice before Hashem your God seven days." This refers to the *Lulav* (palm), the *Aravah* (willows), the *Hadasim* (myrtle), and the *Etrog* (citron)—the four species with which we are to rejoice during the holiday. But if the Four Species constitute an additional aspect of *Sukkot*, why is the holiday still only called "*Sukkot*"? Why not the Feast of the *Lulav*? What is the importance of the *Sukkot*—the booths? And where does this word *Sukkot* come from? Why was it decided that this holiday should occur after *Rosh Hashanah* and *Yom Kippur*? Why not after *Pesach* and *Shavuot*? What is the significance of the Four Species?

We have already learned that the Torah's writings originate in cosmic consciousness, in which a thought develops prior to its physical manifestation. Deciphering the Torah thus helps improve our lives. The Torah itself says, "Therefore choose life." But how are we to do so? By constructing a *Sukkah* in memory of the *Sukkot* erected in the desert? No. The objective here is to create a connection with cosmic events that are happening at a particular moment by means of physical actions or objects. And this is the reason for celebrating *Sukkot*.

Kabbalah teaches that the body has as much significance as the soul. Before we understand the meaning of the holiday, we must therefore understand its material aspect. With regard to the *Sukkah*, we must first understand the physical principle, but we will not stop there. We will also ask why the *Sukkah* is to be built in a specific manner, and what the effect of its shape and dimensions might be.

Before we begin to discuss the *Sukkah* as an instrument for cosmic connection, we should first turn to the segment from the Babylonian Talmud in which a disagreement is described between Rav Eliezer and Rav Akiva. Is the *Sukkah* described in Leviticus physical or merely symbolic, like the protective clouds that accompanied the Israelites in the desert for 40 years? Following that, the Talmud describes how the *Sukkah* is to be built. There is no additional description of the significance of the *Sukkah* beyond what is said in the Torah.

The most important part of the construction of the *Sukkah* is the *Sechach*, or covering. No other kind of covering will do except the *Sechach*, which must be composed of something that once grew from the ground but is no longer attached to it. A shady tree, for example, is not considered *Sechach*. The *Sechach* must also be constructed in such a way that the shadowed area of the *Sukkah* is greater than the non-shadowed area. In building the walls, one may use any material. Two of the walls must be complete and the third may be partial. A fourth wall is not required.

What is going on here? Have the Talmud Sages become building contractors? No, but they knew how to use Kabbalah to develop information according to which we can construct instruments that can connect us to the cosmic events occurring at the same time. During the seven days and nights of the holiday, the *Sukkah* must be considered our main residence, and our regular house must be seen as only a temporary one. Our main meals must therefore be taken in the *Sukkah*, and we must sleep in the *Sukkah* as well.

Once this principle is understood, many people decide to fulfill only part of the tradition. But if one does not observe the totality of the holiday, the cosmic energy begins to weaken, and much of the connection is lost. How can we resolve the apparent contradiction between the preoccupation with the world on *Sukkot*, and the origin of the holiday in the metaphysical cosmic code of the Torah?

Another important aspect of the *Sukkah* is the custom of inviting a different biblical guest on each day of *Sukkot*— a custom that originated with The Ari. These are the *Ushpizin* (special guests invited each day), and the visitors are Abraham, Isaac, Jacob, Moses, Aaron, Joseph, and David. Each guest acts as a chariot for the energy of the particular *Sfirah* connected to each day. There is, in addition, an Aramaic prayer that is recited for each different visitor. Inviting the Ushpizin connects us to them, and with their assistance we better connect to the Light of the Sfirot and to the power of the Clouds of Honor. The Ushpizim help us build the vessel that contains the Light of the Creator, which we will need for an entire year.

After discussing the *Sukkah* and the sitting in it, we arrive at the second important aspect of the holiday: the Four Species. In Leviticus 23:40, it is said, "And you shall take you on the first day the fruit of goodly trees, branches of palm-trees, and boughs of thick trees, and willow of the brook, and ye shall rejoice before Hashem your God seven days." The fruit of goodly trees (citrus) is the *Etrog*; the boughs of thick trees are the *Hadasim*; the branch of a palm tree is the *Lulav*; and the willows of the brook are the Aravot. But why must we take the Four Species, and why must we rejoice with them?

From a technical perspective, the Four Species must be held in the hands of the worshipper during the Hallel service, which is taken from the Book of Psalms, Chapters 113 through 118. We shake them at the beginning of Psalm 118, as well as during the recitation of verse 25 of that same Psalm. The *Lulav* is to be held in the right hand together with the three *Hadasim* and the two Aravot, and the *Etrog* is to be held in the left hand. But what is the purpose of the Four Species? Why were these particular plants chosen and not others? The Ravs called the entire process *Netilat HaLulav*, or the Taking of the *Lulav*. Why is the process not named after the other plants? Are the others secondary in importance?

The Zohar tells how Rav Shimon's pupils met a man in the field who had come to pick a *Lulav* for *Sukkot*. The man asked them about the purpose of the Four Species on *Sukkot*, and Rav Yossi answered that the group had pondered this question but were interested in hearing what he himself thought their purpose might be. The man replied that his teacher, Rav Isaac, had taught him that *Sukkot* is a time for one to become stronger and reinforced in the face of the forces of darkness that have taken over all nations of the world. The Four Species are a symbolic representation of the holy name of the Creator, and only through them can one achieve control.

We activate the software of the *Lulav* so that we are able to connect to the hardware that is *Zeir Anpin*—to the energy reservoir in the personal aspect of the DNA. This form of activation is achieved by "shaking" the bundle of software. These shakings receive messages that are transmitted into space, as would occur with a satellite or an antenna. Through the shakings we improve the reception of our antenna, the Four Species.

When the shakings are performed with the meditations outlined by The Ari, the required connection may be achieved. And there are six directions in which we point the software: east, west, south, north, up, and down. It should be noted that when we discuss directions, we are referring to the thought consciousness that begins and extends in these directions. Therefore, when we speak of the direction south, we are discussing not only the physical direction, but also the "south" that according to the portion of *Va'era* of *The Zohar* is the origin of the thought consciousness called *Chesed*. The *Lulav* connects us to this energy, and this knowledge will assist us in forming the connection with the energy reservoir of *Zeir Anpin* for genetic purposes. Thus, as long as our connection to the energy called *Zeir Anpin* includes six Sfirot or energies, then by means of the shakings the software will be activated. In our minds, the shakings are guided by the thought that in the south we are able to tap into the thought conscious called *Chesed*. We must perform these six cycles, for they represent the composition of *Zeir Anpin*, and our objective is to connect to *Zeir Anpin* and to receive the immense energy. Since *Zeir Anpin* contains these six thought energies, we must direct the physical and metaphysical antennae accordingly. That is how we perform the appropriate connection with *Zeir Anpin*.

We start by directing our software toward the south, while our thoughts are tuned in to *Chesed*. Since initially we are facing east, the south is to our right. After turning to the north, which is *Gvurah*, we will turn back to the east with our thoughts tuned in to the central column, *Tiferet*. These three Sfirot, or energies, form the potential of the upper triangle. To broaden the connection, we tune in to Abraham for the south, Isaac for the north, and Jacob for the east. Thus we form the upper triangle of the Magen David (Star of David), and a protective shield is created. With the software of the four Kingdoms of Life, we have connected to the "Light of Chasadim," which will now be connected to us not only in a metaphysical way, but also on a physical level to protect our physical lives. Even though it is called "potential" thought, we must still introduce this thought into our reality. The fourth shaking, which is directed upward, will in fact be directed with the thought that one must connect to *Netzach*, for which Moses is the chariot. When the shakings are directed downward, while the tip of the *Lulav* still points upward, we connect to *Hod*, the left column, for which Aaron the High Priest is the chariot. The last shaking is to the west, connecting us to *Yesod* and to the chariot of Joseph the Righteous.

The shaking in each direction is actually a combination of three shakes. The act of shaking includes an outward extension of the *Lulav* and its return. This action repeats itself three times in each direction of shaking. Three shakes are in accordance with the basic structure of the three-column system. The thought consciousness required for the use of the Four Species contains an additional dimension that makes use of the letters of the Explicit Name in order to reinforce the action of the Four Species. The first three letters denote right, left, and central columns.

This whole system was designed by Rav Isaac Luria, who studied and extracted it from *The Zohar* to help us reach our goal of "therefore choose life." Using the *Yud Hei Vav Hei* enables us to harness the power of *Zeir Anpin* so that we may remove any obstacle in our physical system and recompose the DNA to ensure that the future is without destruction, despair, or grief. At the same time, however, it is necessary for us to understand how we arrive at each letter and combination, because the greater our knowledge, the better will be our channel to *Zeir Anpin*.

There are two additional aspects of the shakings. One is that the execution of three shakes in each of the six directions creates a set of 18 shakings. In numerology, 18 equals *chai*, ‎חי‎, which means life. The set of shakings injects us with the Life force and connects us to the Tree of Life. The sec-

ond aspect is the integration of the shakings into the Hallel
הלל service; Hallel equals *Adonai* in numerology, which
relates to *Malchut*. The Hallel is also composed of Psalms
written by King David (the chariot to the *Sfirah* of *Malchut*).
The combination of the shakings of the *Lulav* (the communication channel to *Zeir Anpin*) with the Hallel service (the
communication channel to *Malchut*) offers us a great opportunity to unite *Zeir Anpin* and *Malchut* and, having done so,
to establish within ourselves the Creator's power of Light.
This effort is like metaphysical surgery that is performed to
remove spiritual viruses, open up energy blockages, and
repair defects that have developed over the past year in our
spiritual and physical DNA.

We conclude our communication with the Four
Species with the *Hakafot*, in which we walk around in circles
inside the *Sukkah*. This connects us to the surrounding light
from the aspect of *Zeir Anpin* while we are reciting verses
arranged in alphabetic order. These verses also encrypt the
power of the *Yud Hei Vav Hei*, and therefore complete the
action of healing the DNA and reinforcing the immune system.

The Four Species can help us as well as all of mankind.
According to *The Zohar*, the Four Species are a way in which
to receive blessing for the entire year. And if we do not take
advantage of this once-yearly opportunity to attract energy,
The Zohar specifically notes that we will not be able to introduce this energy into our lives.

A Deeper Look at Sukkot

We must clarify the connection between *Pesach*, *Shavuot*, and *Sukkot* in order to truly understand the last of these three holidays. Kabbalistically, the number three symbolizes the three components of all powers of the Creator: right, left, and central columns. *The Zohar* says that each of the three holidays constitutes one component of a single comprehensive energy: *Pesach* is right column, *Shavuot* is central column, and *Sukkot* is left column.

Kabbalah teaches that there is nothing wrong with the desire to receive, and that it is the means by which the Creator's power expresses itself. The Creator had no need to express Himself, but He did have the need to share. In order to share, however, one needs a vessel, which is the thought energy of the desire to receive. Without the desire to receive, the Creator's desire to share cannot manifest.

We should not relinquish the desire to receive; however, during the first ten days of the month of Tishrei, we should consciously transform our desire to receive for the self alone into a desire to receive for the sake of sharing. This transformation creates a circuitry of energy. The location in Jerusalem on which the Holy Temple was built is the strongest point of desire to receive anywhere on earth. But this spot has the innate quality of the desire to receive for the sake of sharing. That is why it is the energy center of the universe.

What is the cosmic time schedule? On the physical level, we see the full moon. But why does this occur on the 15th day of Tishrei? What causes the sun and the moon to be positioned in such a way that the moon appears to be full when viewed from the earth's surface? The Torah's coded answer is as follows: On the 15th day of each month, the moon and the sun meet because there is a perfect union between *Zeir Anpin* and *Malchut*. On this day, *Malchut* uninterruptedly receives energy from the sun, and the sun gives its full strength to the moon. This is the wonderful cosmic event that takes place on the 15th day of each month.

But what is special about the 15th day of Tishrei, as distinct from other months? *Pesach* is celebrated on the 15th day of *Nissan*, but on *Pesach* there was a great outburst of energy that disappeared the next day. Like a hangover after a party, there was energy and now it is gone, and we feel the lack. On *Sukkot* we can connect to energy similar to that of the 15th day of *Nissan*, but we do not want it to disperse; instead, we want to keep it for at least a year. We want to connect to the unification that also occurs on *Pesach*, but with is one major difference: On

Sukkot we maintain this energy as part of our individual universe. On *Pesach*, this cannot be done.

Pesach, the 15th day of *Nissan*, is a wonderful gift—but it is not a gift that we have earned. This gift allowed for the Exodus from Egypt, but according to the concept of Bread of Shame, we have not maintained it. In short, we did not earn the energy of *Pesach*. On *Rosh Hashanah* and *Yom Kippur*, we earn the energy by completely transforming the desire to receive for the self alone into the desire to receive for the sake of sharing—a reversal that we must perform in consciousness. Because of those ten days, the Creator saw fit to inject the world with that same strong energy on *Sukkot*, (the Light of Wisdom) Or *D'Chochmah*, for then there would be a vessel to receive the energy—a vessel that had been refined for ten days.

On *Sukkot* we enter another kingdom in the universe. Unlike *Pesach*, on *Sukkot* we can maintain this energy using the force of restriction—the power of the central column, which was reinforced on the days between *Rosh Hashanah* and *Yom Kippur*. *Sukkot* strengthens the desire to receive and makes it ready to use—for on the ten days between *Rosh Hashanah* and *Yom Kippur*, we build a desire to receive that can deal with high intensities of energy, such as the energy that causes the moon to appear full.

This requires some effort on our part, but the *Sukkah* is not just a tent; it is also a communication system. Talmudic scholars functioned as scientists in determining the physical requirements for the construction of the *Sukkah*. We must understand that the Torah's word *tvezacharta*—"and you shall remember"—is not derived from the word *zikaron*, or memory, but from the word *zachar*, male. And what is the male? He is the leader, the viaduct—he who gives life. The male has sperm and the woman does not. This is not chauvinism; rather, it is a physical phenomenon that indicates a metaphysical source. On *Sukkot* we are able to connect to *Binah* and take as much energy as we wish because we have earned it—and in order to do so, we must build a metaphysical cosmic communication system. But how does the structure of the walls, the trees, and the branches express this metaphysical communication?

What are the cosmic events that caused *The Zohar* to designate *Sukkot* as left column, *Pesach* as right column, and *Shavuot* as central column? As we have seen, the objective on *Rosh Hashanah* was to arrive at the energy storeroom of *Binah*, with the negative side placing obstacles in our way. From *Rosh Hashanah* until *Yom Kippur*, we used the software we received to remove these obstacles and to reach the storeroom. In addition, we learned that in Tishrei we intend to access as much energy as possible; the more energy we connect to, the better our year will be in terms of our physical, mental, and spiritual well-being. The objective is to enlarge the vessel, because the amount of energy we receive depends on the capacity of the vessel, and the capacity of the vessel is relative to the desire to receive.

Hence, the objective of *Sukkot* is to construct channels that will enable the maximum degree of beneficence in the next year. This is a battery that must be charged for an entire year. The 15th day of Tishrei is important because energy is in

abundance; on this day, everything reaches realization and mat-
uration. The harvest is simply a physical expression of a cosmic
state in which the sun and the moon are unified. The sun gives
its full strength to the vessel of the moon, and therefore the
moon appears to be full. On *Sukkot*, which is left column, we are
seeking the energy we require for an entire year. There is only
one way to connect to the energy, and that is through our desire
to receive. But this must be a desire to receive for the sake of
sharing, because that is the only unrestricted way of connecting
to the energy.

On *Pesach*, *The Zohar* alludes to what takes place on the
15th day of *Nissan*. On this day we receive a great thrust of energy without having the opportunity to earn it. In *Nissan*, we do
not have a vessel with sufficient capacity because our desire to
receive for the self alone has not undergone transformation; we
have not earned the cosmic event that created the Exodus from
Egypt. According to *The Zohar*, the Exodus from Egypt was necessary because the Israelites were at the door of the 50th gate of
negativity, which is complete control of the negative side.

On *Pesach*, there is no question of a connective process.
The cosmic event on that day did not require the construction
of a desire to receive for the sake of sharing. On *Pesach* we wish
to liken our form to that of the Light, and this is the concept of
the *matzah*. In the *matzah*, all internal aspects of bread that
manifest the desire to receive for the self alone are canceled. By
eating the *matzah*, we express the similarity in form to the wonderful force that resulted in the Exodus from Egypt.

There are four days between *Yom Kippur* and *Sukkot*. Eevery day in Tishrei is part of the cosmic hardware, and we must therefore understand the meaning of each. In The Ari's *Gate of Meditations*, it is written that during the days between *Yom Kippur* and *Shemini Atzeret* (the Eighth Day of Assembly), everything is directed toward approaching the energy of the right column. By the time of *Yom Kippur*, we have already reprogrammed the desire to receive for the self alone so that it has become a desire to receive for the sake of sharing, and we must now embrace the right column.

The Ari says that the drawing of energy takes place via two parallel channels. The first is directly from *Binah*, and the second is through the sun, through *Zeir Anpin*. We are referring here to the positive energy called Light of Chasadim. The first channel brings this Light in the form of Surrounding Light, which is the DNA of the environmental protection we require. It surrounds the entire universe and shapes our relations with everyone and everything. The second channel brings Inner Light, which reaches us directly and is concerned with our own individual needs. This energy is drawn through *Zeir Anpin*.

All entities have two components—body and soul, internal and external. When we discuss the surrounding Light that controls the environmental DNA, there are two channels that must be dealt with: body and soul. In order for us to create a connection with *Binah*, we must lay the metaphysical cables that will connect us to these two channels. We must therefore find the metaphysical channels and their expression on the physical level. The inner energy of these channels comes from knowledge. If we do not know why these two channels were built, we will not be able to cause energy to flow through them. This can be compared to telephone lines without electrical power: The electrical power is the knowledge, the meditation. The answer can be found in The Ari's *Gate of Meditations*. According to The Ari, the environmental energy from *Binah* will arrive without the construction of any physical channel. The channels for the attraction of this energy are the days between *Yom Kippur* and *Sukkot*. They constitute the channels for the attraction of the environmental energy from *Binah*. The *Sukkah* constitutes the second channel, the physical channel—whose purpose is to draw internal energy from *Binah*.

The Ari provides us with knowledge of the four days between *Yom Kippur* and *Sukkot*. This pause between the holidays is not accidental. In the month of Tishrei, the month of the *Eitanim* (strong), we charge our batteries for the entire year. The month is generally a powerful month. The Ari states that on these four days, we are given the opportunity to create the software that enables us to connect to the environmental kind of Light energy. These days constitute communication channels to Inner Light. Everyone is born with Inner Light, for without it the body could not move. This is the internal energy of the Vessel.

We receive the Inner Light by virtue of the unique power of each day. The four days represent *Keter*, Chochmah, *Binah*, and *Zeir Anpin*. But how do we manifest the energy we have received on these days in order to create a protective shield for the entire year? The answer lies in the *Sukkah*. The *Sukkah* encompasses and surrounds us—and according to The Ari, the *Sukkah* forms the connection with Surrounding Light. Thus, the protective shield is created out of two elements; the first is the four days between *Yom Kippur* and *Sukkot*, and the second is the *Sukkah* itself.

How did The Ari know that the *Sukkah* provides us with such protection? The name given to the *Sukkah* by the Torah offers us deeper insight as to its inner meaning. The Aramaic letters of the word *Sukkah*, ‏ה כ ו ס‎, are a combination of ‏ו כ‎ (= 26) and ‏ס ה‎ (= 65). Their total numerical value is 91, which is also the total numerical value of the letters of the word *Amen*, a combination of the *Yud Hei Vav Hei* (= 26) representing *Zeir Anpin*, and *Adonai* (= 65), a unification of heaven and earth. This is exactly what we require: We need to take the Inner universe and connect it to the exterior universe, for only in this way will we ensure peripheral protection. After we have consolidated the Inner Light, the instrument that must cope with the great energy of the environmental DNA during the four days, we reach the fifth day—the day that represents *Malchut*. It is then that we begin to use the *Sukkah*. By means of the *Sukkah*'s energy, we draw Surrounding Light and physically form the protective shield.

Now we can understand why the *Sechach*—the roof of the *Sukkah*—must be built in a way that lets us see the stars. We must unify our own personal world with the outer reaches of space. This is the meaning of the *Sukkah*: By watching the stars, we create the cosmic connection. The stars are not just meaningless celestial bodies.

Science asserts that certain stars have already ceased to exist, though their light is reaching us only now. Kabbalah, however, teaches that these stars have returned to their potential state because they have already fulfilled their function. Every star has a purpose. According to *The Zohar*, no leaf or blade of grass can grow without the Light of its individual star. When we watch the stars, we form a connection with the universe. This is the reason for the special requirement of the *Sechach*.

We must use cut-off branches and not paper, metal, or other raw materials. The trees of the *Sechach* must no longer be connected to the ground in order for them to be separated from *Malchut*, which is the desire to receive. The connection that must be made is that between the desire to receive and *Zeir Anpin*, which is the *Sukkah*.

Trees grow upward, against the force of gravity, because they have an inner force that intends to disconnect itself from *Malchut*. Within them is a power of giving, of *Zeir Anpin*. In fact, as long as the branches covering the *Sukkah* are connected to the tree and through it to the ground, they have the internal energy of the desire to receive for the sake of sharing. The walls of the *Sukkah* are considered *Malchut*, since they are connected to the ground. But because the branches of the *Sechach* are independent and do not grow out of the *Sukkah* or the ground, they possess a different internal energy. The Talmudic scholars designed this software thoroughly and carefully, for we are dealing with very serious issues. Environmental protection should not be left to today's scientists. We can do a better job.

What caused such an abundance of Light to be revealed on the 15th day of Tishrei? By understanding this, we can connect to cosmic influences in the strongest possible way. Exodus 13:21 reads, "And Hashem went before them by day in a pillar of cloud, to lead them the way; and by night in a pillar of fire, to give them light; that they might go by day and by night." *The Zohar* explains that the word for pillar, *amud*, is a physical realization of the chariots of the *Shechinah* (the Divine Presence): that is, the three Patriarchs and David. In the above verse, God represents the Light. The words "went before them by day" represent Abraham, with "day" representing the right column. Isaac is represented by the words "in a pillar of cloud"; Jacob is represented by the words "to lead them"; and David by the words "and by night in a pillar of fire." These four created the protective power of the pillar so that the Israelites could proceed safely. *The Zohar* asks why the Israelites had to walk both by day and by night. What were they running from? Was there no Creator there to protect them? The intention of the biblical description is to create a feeling of general harmony, so that the unification of the energies of judgment and of mercy, represented by the day and the night, could takes place.

Rav Abraham Ibn Ezra noted that the pillar of cloud extends from heaven to earth like a line. The Israelites saw the metaphysical energy realize in the world in the shape of this physical miracle. According to Ibn Ezra, the purpose of this was to show that by activating the three forces represented by Abraham, Isaac, and Jacob, there could be a realization of the metaphysical in the physical world. In this way, the Torah tells us that what we realize in the spiritual world will eventually receive physical expression.

In Exodus 13, we saw that the pillar of cloud and the pillar of fire advanced in front of the people; the entire nation could see them. But in Chapter 14, verse 10, it is written, "And when Pharaoh drew nigh, the children of Israel lifted up their eyes, and, behold, the Egyptians were marching after them; and they were so afraid; and the children of Israel cried out unto Hashem." How could the nation that experienced the Exodus from Egypt and later saw the pillars of cloud and fire be so afraid? Had they already forgotten the Exodus from Egypt? How could they be afraid of Pharaoh while the pillars stood before them? The reason for this is that the desire to receive for the self alone creates limitations.

The story of the Exodus from Egypt therefore tells us that the Israelites were preoccupied with the desire to receive for the self alone. Without the infusion of energy by the Creator, the Exodus from Egypt would never have taken place. On the other hand, *Rosh Hashanah* and *Yom Kippur* show us that when we convert the desire to receive for the self alone into the desire to receive for the sake of sharing, our ability to receive energy broadens. And the greater the conversion, the more energy we can access from the energy storehouse of *Binah*.

So the pillars construct the metaphysical channels. But the desire to receive for the self alone restricts the connection.

In Exodus 14:11, it is written, "And they said unto Moses:

'Because there were no graves in Egypt, you have taken us away to die in the wilderness? Wherefore you have dealt this with us, to bring us forth out of Egypt?'" It is amazing to see how a nation that has experienced a great many miracles is so limited by the desire to receive for the self alone. Verse 19 reads,

"And the angel of God, who went before the camp of Israel, removed and went behind them; and the pillar of cloud removed from before them, and stood behind them." The low consciousness of the Israelites at the time of the Exodus from Egypt, as well as the illusory power of the desire to receive for the self alone, caused the apparent disappearance of the pillar of cloud. This illusion led them to believe that they would be better off returning to slavery, without obligations or responsibilities, than living a life of free choice.

Rashi, the great interpreter of the Torah, also interpreted the concept of the pillar of cloud, teaching that the Creator housed the Israelites in *Sukkot* when He led them out of Egypt. This does not refer to physical booths, but rather to the metaphysical Clouds of Honor, which protected the Israelites from the strong sun of the desert. Thus, Rashi forms a kind of connection between the physical and the metaphysical. The Ramban, a well-known kabbalist, accepted this interpretation but went on to say that the Clouds of Honor are a symbol of divine protection—the Divine Light, the power of the three fundamental energies. This power creates a protective cover so that death, represented by the Egyptians, is not able to penetrate. This is the power of the covering laid on the *Sukkot*.

The *Sechach* was built using sophisticated technology with the objective of connecting to the Light. Numbers 9:15 tells us, "On the day that the Tabernacle was reared, the cloud covered the tabernacle." The cloud protected the Tabernacle, and when the cloud was lifted, the people knew they must continue their journey. That is why the holiday of *Sukkot* is connected to joy. No other holiday can so strongly express the connection with the Creator, represented by the cloud that accompanied the Israelites to protect them. This, then, is the connection between the *Sukkah* and the Exodus from Egypt. The objective of the holiday is not to recall the suffering of the Israelites or to pity them. The objective is to fulfill our need for the *Sukkah*—for it is the only way to connect to the cloud that provided the Israelites with protection.

When King Solomon built The Temple, he chose to inaugurate it on *Sukkot*. It is written in Kings I, 8:65, "So Solomon held the feast at that time, and all Israel with him, a great congregation, from the entrance of Hamath unto the Brook of Egypt, before Hashem our God, seven days and seven days, even fourteen days." The first seven days were for the inauguration, and the additional seven were for *Sukkot*. The inauguration festivities took place from the 8th to the 14th day of Tishrei and included *Yom Kippur* as well. From the 15th day of the month until the 21st, *Sukkot* was celebrated.

Even after King Solomon had completed the construction of The Temple, he seemed to be troubled by doubts as to what The Temple could accomplish. In Chapter 8, verse 27, it is written: "But will God in very truth dwell on the earth? Behold, heaven and the heaven of heavens cannot contain Thee; how much less this house that I have built!"

We could raise similar doubts on the subject of *Sukkot*. Is the structure in our yard capable of containing the enormous energy it is supposed to attract? Just like the Holy Temple and the Ark, the *Sukkah* is designed to attract the Creator's Light that exists in the universe.

Why did Solomon choose *Sukkot* for the inauguration of The Temple? Perhaps he wanted to take advantage of the fact that on *Sukkot* people go up to Jerusalem anyway, and that this would be an opportunity for the people to see the wonderful house that King Solomon built. But in his infinite wisdom, King Solomon knew that the focus was not on the physical reality. We saw that King Solomon questioned The Temple's capacity to contain the Light of the Creator.

So why did he build The Temple in the first place? This apparent contradiction teaches us about reality. There are in fact two realities: the authentic one, which is *Zeir Anpin*, and the illusory one of *Malchut*. King Solomon tried to clarify this. These two realities are both essential to the forming of a connection, but they constitute separate channels.

The Temple itself was not the connection; instead, it was a necessary material entity. In order to connect heaven and earth as they were connected in Genesis 1, we need a "telephone line," which is the physical Temple. But King Solomon warned us that the physical aspect is not an end but only a means of connecting with the Light. The main part of the system is the energy consciousness that is injected into the physical conductor. The physical means must be injected with the correct meditation, which is based on the knowledge of the inner and true meaning of the *Sukkah*. Without this knowledge, the connection does not take place—and then, as King Solomon said, the vessel will "not contain Thee."

Deuteronomy clearly states that we must fast on *Yom Kippur*. But if this is the case, why did King Solomon, the wisest of all men, celebrate on that day? Rashi says that during the inauguration, people ate and drank on *Yom Kippur*. Did he lead all of Israel to sin? Did King Solomon compromise the Israelites' connection with *Binah*? Should he thus be considered as "one who causes many to sin?" Why do none of the Torah's commentators condemn King Solomon for this act?

Solomon was familiar both with Tishrei's power and with The Temple's capacity to attract Light by virtue of the Ark within it. This Ark is able to attract the raw energy of the universe as no other physical instrument can. The Ark directed life to The Temple. We need a 15-day purification process, which includes *Rosh Hashanah* and *Yom Kippur*, before we connect to the power of *Binah* on the holiday of *Sukkot*. King Solomon's Temple was an immediate connection to the energy of *Binah*.

There was no need to wait 15 days, and there was no need for the *Yom Kippur* process. It was possible to celebrate before that, for the connection with *Binah* already existed. Therefore, there are no contradictions in King Solomon's actions.

We now wish to ask why the 15th day of Tishrei was chosen to be the day on which the connection with *Binah* occurs. Why is it on that day that we connect to the Clouds of Honor? On this day, according to The Ari, two powers of the Creator appear: internal and peripheral, internal and external—both of which are aspects of *Binah*. Following the four days between *Yom Kippur* and *Sukkot*, which are Keter, Chochmah, *Binah*, and *Zeir Anpin*, we arrive at the day of *Malchut*. Only on the day of *Malchut* can the Inner Light, the vessel for containing the immense energy of *Binah*, be revealed. And only after the construction of the vessel can the peripheral Light—the protective shield of *Binah*—be revealed as well.

In order to better understand the words of The Ari regarding the meaning of the 15th day of Tishrei, we must discuss yet another issue. We know that King Solomon removed the Ark from the City of David, otherwise known as Zion. But what does this mean? *The Zohar* quotes from Psalms 50:2: "Out of Zion, the perfection of beauty, God hath shone forth." The Creator started the world at Zion, which is *Yesod*. Zion is the energy center of the universe; this is where the world began and from which it is nourished. But what is the difference between Zion and Jerusalem? Jerusalem constitutes a channel for the energy of judgment, or *Malchut*, while Zion constitutes a channel for mercy, the aspect of sharing. King Solomon unified these two aspects—the Light known as Zion and the Vessel called Jerusalem—into a channel for the unified power of the Creator. This is the *Sukkah* of Peace that is mentioned in *The Zohar*. The *Sukkah*, by virtue of the branches covering it, manifests the aspect of *Yesod*. Together with the walls that are connected to the ground, which are *Malchut*, we form in our little temple the unification that King Solomon performed between Zion and Jerusalem: the unification of the universe.

This is what occurs on *Sukkot*. The Inner Light that began on the 11th day of Tishrei reaches its destination on the 15th. On that day, the Surrounding Light begins, with the first day being *Chesed* of Surrounding Light. *Chesed* is the seed, the first day of Creation. Genesis 1 reads, "And there was evening and there was morning, day one." Note that it does not say first, but one unification. This is the power of the first day of *Sukkot*, which is connected to Abraham. This is the seed for the week in which we attract Surrounding Light. On this day, Surrounding Light and Inner Light—Zion and Jerusalem—are unified. And that is why King Solomon chose this day for The Temple's inauguration—it suited the grand plan of Genesis. King Solomon knew that Zion and Jerusalem would unify on the inauguration day of The Temple so that people would be able to rejoice, even on *Yom Kippur*.

Sukkot is the holiday that is dedicated to constructing the spiritual vessel. This vessel, which is intended to contain the Light of Wisdom we draw from the reservoir of cosmic energy, is itself made of energy called the Light of Chasadim. The main property of the energy of *Chesed* is conductivity. In the physical world, the energy of *Chesed* is expressed through the most abundant substance on earth: water. The electrical conductivity of sea water is even greater than that of steel or copper electrical cables. Water transmits all the energy invested in it by the power source and does not reserve any for itself. Therefore, water is not damaged when an electrical current flows through it. In order to handle an infinite supply of energy without being harmed, we must thus learn how to nurture the attribute of *Chesed* within us and be in a state of sharing and constant concern for others as well as for the entire universe. The reason people experience a short circuit when an abundance of energy flows through them lies in the desire to receive for the self alone, which creates a blockage and causes energy to accumulate in the body. If we waive the desire to receive and exchange it for perfect conductivity—also known as the desire to share—we are guaranteed no harm in the revelation of Light.

The principle of structural similarity between the human body and the world described by *The Zohar* explains that just as the majority of the surface of the earth is covered with water, so too is the majority of the human body made of water. Why is water so essential to the existence of all life forms? The reason is rooted in the thought consciousness that water expresses in the world: the consciousness of *Chesed*. *Chesed*, sharing and conductivity, are the attributes essential to the revelation of the Light of the Creator in the world. But this Light cannot be directly observed, for it is concealed. Thus, the only way one can know the presence of Light is by indirect means—through a medium of one sort or another that conducts the Light and reveals the potential embodied within it. In order to make use of the power produced by the electrical company's power plant, it is necessary for us to establish a network of consumers and, having done so, to connect a variety of appliances to the network—such as refrigerators, ovens, air conditioners, computers, light fixtures, and motors—that detect the potential embedded in the electricity. In a similar manner, water is the means for the revelation of the Creator's power of Light in the world. The thought consciousness of water is conductivity and sharing—just like the power of Light. This is also why earthly existence requires the presence of water.

When the world was created, the entire surface of the earth was covered with water. *Chesed* ruled throughout, and the Creator's power of Light was unadulterated. Later, the water gathered and land was exposed. This situation found expression in man as well. Upon being created, man totally conducted the Creator's Light; after the Sin, some of this ability and consciousness was lost. This loss is the opening through which chaos penetrated the world. Our spiritual mission in the world, together with acts of sharing, such as tithing and charity, was intended to complete the lack that resulted from the Original Sin of Adam—the consequence of which is a closing of the cracks in our spiritual protection system, ensuring the continuity of revelation of Light in our lives. This is the power or blessing that stems from sharing, and it is the reason that charity saves one from death. The amplification of the Light of Chasadim is therefore the key to the realization of the resurrection of the dead and the removal of death forever. *Sukkot* is a cosmic opportunity that enables us, once a year, to charge ourselves with the Light of Chasadim and, by that means, share a similarity of form with the

Creator and discover a force of infinite sharing in the world. Therefore, particularly during *Sukkot*, it is worth being in a consciousness of giving and concern for others. In this way, we will complete the *Chesed* we are missing and reach a state in which we achieve mind over matter, the resurrection of the dead, and the removal of death forever.

A question is raised by Kings I, 8:2: "And all the men of Israel assembled themselves unto King Solomon at the feast, in the month of *Eitanim*." What is *Eitanim*? Exodus 14:27 reads, "And Moses stretched forth his hand over the sea, and the sea returned to its strength when the morning appeared" (in Aramaic). A change of letters in the word לְאֵיתָנוֹ (*le'eitano*, or "to its strength") produces the word לִתְנָאָיו (*le'tena'av*, "to its conditions")—that is, "to its original properties." The month of *Eitanim* is therefore a month during which we have the ability to perform *Teshuvah*—to return to the origin, to the seed, to connect to our primal essence.

The word *Eitanim* denotes power to return to the "beginning of all beginnings"—to the core, to the seed. This is the power with which King Solomon proclaimed that celebration is acceptable on *Yom Kippur*. Today, we have no Temple and no Ark, but we do have the *Sukkah* to attract environmental protection. We do not celebrate on *Yom Kippur*—only King Solomon could do that—but on *Sukkot* we have the opportunity to attract the immense Light that we toiled to attain on *Rosh Hashanah* and on *Yom Kippur*.

The Zohar, in the portion of Emor, tells us that we must sit in the *Sukkah* for seven days. This is because seven clouds of mercy are connected to the seven Sfirot: *Chesed, Gvurah, Tiferet, Netzach, Hod, Yesod,* and *Malchut.* These clouds of surrounding Light cover us when we are in the *Sukkah.* If we have attained a high level of consciousness, these seven clouds unify us with King Solomon, together with The Temple and the Ark. When all seven clouds manifest on the seventh day, the day of *Malchut,* then the power of Jerusalem is revealed. *Malchut* connects with *Yesod.* That is why we sit in the *Sukkah* for seven days.

What is the internal energy that has brought such attention to the clouds of honor? Why do all five books of the Torah emphasize the significance of the clouds? Let us recall what is written in Numbers 9:15-19:

> And on the day that the tabernacle was reared the cloud covered the Tabernacle, even the Tent of the Testimony; and at even there was upon the Tabernacle as it were the appearance of fire, until morning. So it was always: the cloud covered it, and the appearance of fire by night. And whenever the cloud was taken up from over the Tent, then after that the children of Israel journeyed; and in the place where the cloud abode, there the children of Israel encamped. At the commandment of Hashem the children of Israel journeyed, and at the commandment of Hashem they encamped: as long as the cloud abode upon the tabernacle they remained encamped. And when the cloud tarried

upon the tabernacle many days, then the children of
Israel kept the charge of Hashem, and journeyed not.

Is this story relevant to us today, even though the
Tabernacle no longer exists? Aaron, who was the cloud of
Chesed, created unity among all seven clouds. That is why we sit
in the *Sukkah* for seven days. *Chesed* is the inner energy of the
cloud. The cloud rests on the Tabernacle during the day. The Ari
interprets the word *yom* (day) as *Chesed* and thus draws the connection between the holiday of *Sukkot* and the Clouds of Honor.
But this connection cannot be made only by means of the desire
to receive. Even turning the desire to receive for oneself into the
desire to receive for the sake of sharing is not enough.

A connection to the Creator's Light can be achieved only
by connecting to the energy of the right column, the power of
Chesed—a pure force that was never a desire to receive. The
desire to share is infinite and preceded the formation of the
desire to receive. Therefore, we must firmly establish the channels to the positive energy so as to attract the Light. Indeed, we
must at the same time transform the desire to receive for the self
alone into the desire to receive for the sake of sharing—and that
is what is accomplished on *Rosh Hashanah* and *Yom Kippur*. But
in order to receive the energy, we must connect to the channels
that lead to the right column, to the pure Light.

How can we this create this connection to the Light for
ourselves? The *Sukkah*, with all its building instructions, is the
way in which to connect. We create a physical Tabernacle, and
even though we might not see the cloud, it is there. We can also

connect to the Ark once a year, every year. We cannot maintain the permanent connection with the Light that existed in The Temple, but for seven days the *Sukkah* connects us to *Binah* even without The Temple.

The Sages discussed this verse from Leviticus: "I made the children of Israel dwell in booths." Does this refer to physical or metaphysical *Sukkot*? Rav Eliezer claims that the *Sukkot* were not physical, and that their purpose was only to connect to the Clouds of Honor. Rashi and Rav Akiva, however, say that the *Sukkot* were physical entities intended for protection from the sun. All the Sages attribute great importance to the holiday of *Sukkot* and to the connection to the Clouds of Honor. The *Sukkah* is the physical realization of The Temple and the Ark within it.

The Zohar, in the portion of Pikudei, explains that the cornerstones of Jerusalem and Zion never fell into the hands of the various nations who conquered the city. The stones were not burned; they were preserved by the Creator without losing even a single pebble. And when the Creator decides to rebuild Jerusalem, the old stones will be returned to their places, and the Evil Eye will no longer govern them. Then we will be able to see the actualization of the return of the nation.

The necessary result of this is immortality, which is simply a reemergence of the removal of death forever. The forces of darkness will be defeated once and for all. This is the power of the *Sukkah*. Simply by sitting in the *Sukkah*, we connect with *Binah* and the Clouds of Honor.

According to The Ari, in *Gate of Meditations*, the purpose of the *Lulav* and the Four Species is to induce the seven stages of Chasadim of Inner Light. This is the Light that comes from *Zeir Anpin*, which deals with inner, individual DNA. Contrary to the medical doctrine which claims that the DNA is unchanging, The Ari teaches us that DNA is changed each year by the kind of energy that reaches it. The Four Species do not influence the general environmental DNA as the *Sukkah* does; rather, they affect the personal DNA. They enable *Zeir Anpin*, with all of its blessings, to influence our genetic code. Thus we can change the features we were born with. We must therefore identify the channels for attracting this energy so that we can use them.

The Ari says that each day we must shake the Four Species, and in this way arouse the Light of Mercy. Just as the *Sukkah* is a means of attracting environmental protection, so too can the Four Species assist in attracting physical and mental health to our individual DNA. And just as the *Sukkah* attracts a different aspect of the Light of *Binah* each day, so too can the Four Species attract a different aspect of the Light of *Zeir Anpin* each day. The influence of the Light that stems from *Zeir Anpin* lies in the realm of the individual DNA. Essentially, we are changing the script of life on a personal level.

This is something that lies beyond holistic medicine or homeopathy, which are, to be sure, essential as well. But there is an additional element pertaining to *tikkun*, or correction. There are situations in which even natural medicine and the strongest will to survive and heal are not sufficient to overcome sickness. Therefore, according to Kabbalah's decoding of the Torah, this season of *Sukkot*—and in particular the Four Species, which are in fact medicinal plants—will help us overcome any sickness contained in the DNA, including illnesses that would only be discovered 20 years from now. We are capable of making the genetic change now. We can modify the defect in the individual and general DNA not only in the fetal state, but in adulthood as well.

Those well versed in kabbalistic thought know that the *Yud Hei Vav Hei* best represents the power of the Creator on the material level. There are four letters in the Name, and the Four Species are associated with the letters of the Name. The Four Species were selected so that at this particular time of year, they can constitute the strongest channels to the energy, and in this way express the power of the Creator on the most potent physical level.

But why these four particular species and not others? According to The Ari, the myrtle represents *Chesed*, the right column. Myrtles have three leaves. The entire length of the myrtle branch has three leaves originating from a single point. The myrtle is connected to the letter *Yud* of the *Yud Hei Vav Hei*, which is Chochmah—and Chochmah is the energy of sharing.

The myrtle, therefore, is the energy of sharing. *The Zohar* tells us to take three branches of myrtles and tie them together into one unit. This unity represents *Chesed*, *Gvurah*, and *Tiferet*, the upper triangle of the Magen David, our shield on the personal level. The myrtle itself has three leaves originating from a single point so as to show the complete and unified internal energy of the *hadas* (myrtle)—the unity of the three energies of *Chesed*, *Gvurah* and *Tiferet*.

This is why the myrtle was chosen. It is not mere tradition. The Ari used the *hadas* throughout the entire year, on Shabbat eve and Shabbat morning, for its pleasing fragrance—but according to *The Zohar*, the myrtle could not be used throughout the year for the same purpose as that for which it is used on *Sukkot*. Smelling the myrtle during the year has a certain restricted ability to attract Light, but its real power of attraction can occur only on *Sukkot*.

Today, modern medicine deals exclusively with symptoms. Yet physicians concede that almost all sicknesses originate from psychosomatic causes. Modern medications do not possess the thought that is capable of healing. Kabbalah does not use medications or natural healing. Instead, it focuses directly on the cause, at the DNA level. We prefer to heal illnesses before they appear. As it is said in the Torah, "Therefore choose life." Science says that our life's course is determined by the time we are born. The difference between life and death—between blessing and curse—depends on whether we choose to connect to the Light. We can either eliminate the illness at its root or, heaven forbid, forfeit the connection to the Light and enable chaos to manifest itself in the world.

Simchat Beit
HASHO'EVAH

The framework of *Sukkot* includes *Simchat Beit Hasho'evah*, the celebration of the drawing water or the libation. In observance of *Simchat Beit Hasho'evah*, people pour water from one vessel to another in a spirit of enjoyment and rejoicing.

What is the significance of the holiday? Kabbalah teaches us that tradition alone has no independent significance, but a coded meaning is hidden in tradition, and that meaning is what our study uncovers. Regarding *Simchat Beit Hasho'evah*, it is written in the Talmud, "He who did not see the jubilation of *Beit Hasho'evah* never saw jubilation in his life." Surely we have all experienced joy to some degree, but few of us have had the good fortune to experience lasting joy. *Simchat Beit Hasho'evah* provides us with a year's worth of joy in just one day! It is complete joy—joy even greater than that experienced on *Simchat Torah*.

In order to understand this, we must seek the encrypted meaning of the sacred writings. In the Torah it is written
va'nizkarta ("and you will recall"), and in *The Zohar* it is written *va'nizkerem* ("and we will remember them"), indicating
that our ancestors poured water on the altar. But what did
the Talmud mean by *Simchat Beit Hasho'evah*? Was the rejoicing only in the *sho'evah*? And what does shoe'vah (libation)
mean? Does it mean nothing more than drawing water so
that we will have a happier year? And if this is indeed its full
interpretation, then what is the connection between water
and joy? In general, what is joy, and what is the guarantee
that we will feel it?

Additional pieces of the puzzle are found in *The Zohar*,
in the portion of *Pinchas*, concerning the end of the Flood.
The Zohar explains that in the course of the month of Tishrei,
the flood waters gradually diminished, and eventually, on
Sukkot, the Ark came to rest on the mountain of Ararat.
During the time of The Temple, the holiday included a sacrifice of 70 oxen for the 70 ministers who were in charge of
all nations. Thirteen oxen were sacrificed on the first day, 12
on the second day, 11 on the third, and so on, until the seventh and final day. Why was this done? What is the connection between this tradition, the Flood, and the puzzle of
Simchat Beit Hasho'evah?

According to *The Zohar*, sacrificing 70 oxen brought
peace and prosperity to the entire world. What is the connection between sacrifices and world peace? As long as The
Temple existed, before the Israelites went astray, there was

peace in the world—something that eludes us today. A study published in Time magazine showed that during the past 100 years there have been an average of 36 wars per year somewhere in the world. Just as there are 36 righteous men in the world, so it seems that there must be 36 wars in the world. And today, of course, there are still wars taking place. How could there have been peace throughout the entire world during the time of The Temple?

The Zohar answers these questions, one by one. First, it explains that the entire biblical story of the Flood is a coded allegory describing a spiritual reality that recurs every year throughout the universe. The Ark was not just a ship and the Flood was not just a heavy rain. The month of Tishrei, the seventh month of the year, is a time during which the Shechinah comes to rest upon Israel, when the Light of Binah is revealed in the world. This is the reason for the complex system of Tishrei holidays. First we purify our spiritual vessel, and then we overcome the hurdles and arrive at the energy reservoir of Binah. Finally, we connect to this Light and absorb it into our lives by means of the Sukkah and the Four Species.

The Sukkah connects us to Binah, the Lulav to Zeir Anpin, and the Etrog to Malchut. During the Flood, the raging waters expressed the chaos and negativity that humanity's actions had propagated throughout the universe. In the month of Tishrei, the Light of Binah gradually removes the darkness. During the Flood, this was expressed by the receding of the waters, which represents the removal of chaos.

The Zohar explains that every year, the revelation of the Light during the month of Tishrei causes the sins of Israel to diminish—and along with this, the number of angels of destruction in the world also decreases. Since sacrifices not only nourish mankind but also remove judgment and negativity, it is now clear why the ancient sacrifices also gradually lessened during *Sukkot*.

But an additional point must be made with regard to this matter. All those who think that feeding the nations of the world can solve our problems are both misled and misleading. *The Zohar* tells us that only the Israelites—people who understand and work with the spiritual laws of the universe as dictated by Kabbalah—can provide the nations of the world with the spiritual sustenance necessary for their existence. Unfortunately, the Israelites have turned their backs on the Light and have disavowed the cosmic responsibility that has been imposed on them for the past 3,400 years. Their thinking was, "I must look after myself, so why must I take care of others?"

Kabbalah teaches that it is always essential to share with others. What does sharing mean? In order to be connected to the Light, one must act like the Light. And Light knows only one thing: sharing. Therefore, whoever wishes to be connected to the Light must not only receive, but receive for the sake of sharing. In the times of The Temple, during *Sukkot*, the Israelite people provided Light and fulfillment to the 70 nations. In connection with this, *The Zohar* poses some very interesting questions: Is it possible that the nations do not want this? What happens if they do not have the appropriate vessels to contain the Light with which we provide them?

These questions are especially important in light of the fact that most people do not even know that they can receive the fulfillment, their spiritual food, only from the Israelites. It is written in *The Zohar* that there is no joy for the 70 angels responsible for the 70 nations. *The Zohar* is revealing two facts here. First, we are not instructed to approach a non-Israelite and say, "Listen, I want to provide you with spiritual sustenance." At best, he will politely say thank you—but will he even understand the significance of this statement? Second, *The Zohar* reveals that we should "speak directly with the overseeing angels." Each nation has an angel appointed as its spiritual minister. When the governing angels are satisfied on *Sukkot*, there is no greater joy in the world. By causing this to happen during the seven days of *Sukkot*, we solve the problem of chaos for the entire world.

The nations of the world are becoming increasingly aware of *The Zohar*'s power. If only everyone would begin to understand the power of *The Zohar*! When The Temple existed, there were no fears in the world, and no one was afraid of foreign nations waging war. Only under such peaceful conditions can complete joy be experienced. True joy requires freedom from chaos, a condition in which a people can live quietly and not be concerned about violence or unexpected misfortune. All those who are connected to the Light and who perform the act of propagating the Light of

Sukkot are ensuring that the Light force of the Creator will bring about peace and joy throughout the world.

As the Light of *Binah* brings rest to the judgments, we say, "and the Ark rested" (vatanach, from the word menuchah, to rest). Precisely at this moment, when the world is liberated and freed of chaos, *Simchat Beit Hasho'evah* takes place. Here, for the first time, we learn the meaning of true happiness. Complete and eternal joy means total freedom from chaos, as it is written: "He will swallow up death forever." This is revealed in the universe during *Simchat Beit Hasho'evah*, and we connect to this energy by pouring water and drawing it from the well. As *The Zohar* explains, the well is the Torah, our connection to the Tree of Life—and the water is the Vessel that conducts the Light of Chasadim in the world.

This consciousness reveals the Creator's power of Light in *Malchut*. Therefore, as long as we still share similarity of form with the Light, we conduct the Light force of the Creator inherent in the Torah, and we reveal it in the world by means of *Chesed*. We are therefore free of chaos and are granted true and endless joy. Ignorance of the nuances of the Torah is a sure recipe for chaos. Knowledge, on the other hand, propagates the Light and removes chaos. This secret can be learned only from *The Zohar*, which is the sole means of removing chaos from the universe. One hour of studying *The Zohar* is equivalent to an entire year of studying other spiritual texts.

For 2,000 years, people have been studying the Mishnah and *Gemara* but have scarcely even touched Kabbalah. Consequently, wc have suffered 2,000 years of exile and destruction. The time has come to switch from the losing horse to the winning horse. According to the Talmud, all other regular celebrations with which we are familiar, including *Simchat Torah* (the holiday where we dance with the Torah), do not change reality or solve problems, but bring about only temporary relief.

When the Talmud scholars said *sho'evah*, they were referring to the action of drawing the 70 appointed angels, when we invite them to come to us in order to receive the spiritual supply allocated to them. This is why the holiday is called *Simchat Beit Hasho'evah*, the Celebration of the Water Drawing.

Just as *Sukkot* is connected to water, so too is it connected to *Chesed*, the power of mercy and kindness. Why is this so? In order to uncover the Light of Chochmah in the world, it is necessary to cover it with an instrument called the Light of Chasadim. During *Sukkot*, we equip ourselves with an overflowing amount of Light of Chasadim. Therefore, we pour as much water as we can. In the course of pouring the well water from a pitcher into a bowl, we draw the Light of life and consciousness of *Chesed* into our lives and propagate it to all corners of the universe.

The bowl is a symbol of each and every one of us. The water being poured into the bowl conducts the abundance to us and to the entire world. The pouring of the water with the right consciousness as a sequel to all other communications of *Sukkot* allows for the nourishment of the world's nations with Light, the elimination of chaos, and the bringing of true joy to all mankind. Those who perform these actions will thus have the good fortune of protection from negativity.

In order to accomplish this, however, we must take responsibility for the propagation of Light. Mutual responsibility means thinking of others—Israelite or otherwise—and sharing the power of the Light with them. Unlike a black hole, which draws in everything around it, we draw during *Simchat Beit Hasho'evah* in order to give satisfaction to all the governing angels. *The Zohar* says that in our times we will encounter people in Europe, Israel, and elsewhere who do not want to be connected to the Light, and who are not interested in sharing with others. *Simchat Beit Hasho'evah* teaches us that it is not enough to share the Light with our loved ones, but that it must be shared with every living person.

This is our personal responsibility, and it is the reason The Kabbalah Centre undertook the mission of sharing and distributing *The Zohar* throughout the world. As a well-known part of this effort, hundreds of copies of *The Zohar* have been distributed in Iran. This action benefits the Iranian people in that it can help curb Iranian aggression and even prevent world war in a much more efficient manner than could a military operation. For decades, the Iranians have made trouble for the entire world and continue to do so until this very day. If they do not receive the spiritual fulfillment that they deserve, they will suffer, and the world will suffer along with them. But if we channel the Light force of the Creator wisely, revealing it in the world in a balanced manner and out of concern for the true needs of others, then we will be able to exchange the prophecy of fury with a more positive cassette.

The Zohar tells us that Moses spoke with Rav Shimon and specifically told him that in the days of the Messiah—and there is no question that we are in this period now—only *The Zohar* could save the world and take it from Tree of Knowledge of Good and Evil consciousness to Tree of Life consciousness. For 2,000 years, the illusory political game has not helped anyone. Politicians say one thing today and say another tomorrow; today this one is in power and tomorrow someone else will be in control. But the bottom line is this: As long as there is no peace in Israel, there cannot be peace anywhere else in the world. In order to spread the Light and bring peace to the entire world, all the People of Israel must gather in Israel by means of the consciousness taught by *The Zohar*, and in this way Light will be channeled to the world. Israelites are not needed abroad. The People of Israel should dwell in the Land of Israel, from whence spiritual abundance can be sent to the entire world. In Israel, everyone draws from the energy center that is there. The reason there is emigration from Israel is that without a worthy spiritual vessel, it is impossible to endure the power and energy that prevail there. Those who emigrate find their own excuse, but the root of the problem is quite different. The problem lies instead in the immense power that resides in the

Land of Israel. Those who do not know how to cope with the Light choose to leave, and those who choose to stay do so because the Light does not bother them.

The number of excuses for moving away from the Light exceeds the number of people in the world. The *Gemara* states that 1,000 enter, but only one leaves with the Light. Tens of thousands of new students come to The Kabbalah Centre each year; hundreds of staff and volunteers share the Light every day, and this activity is ever-growing. We do not have reservations about any person in the world. The time has thus come for everyone to speak of *The Zohar*. With God's help, learning from *The Zohar* and the Light revealed in the universe during *Simchat Beit Hasho'evah* gives us the good fortune to solve and uproot all manifestations of chaos. *Bila Hamavet Lanetzach* (immortality) is possible, and we can expect to see true and lasting joy for the entire world.

Hoshana
RABA

oshana Raba is a connection that involves life and death. On this night you combine seeing your shadow, which represents a view into your life and all the energy it includes, with the reading of the book of Deuteronomy from the Torah.

We're fortunate to live in a time when advanced technologies are becoming the norm. We're used to thinking beyond the limits of our five senses—and one purpose of our work at the Kabbalah Centre is to help develop that ability and put it to use. By seeing your shadow against the backdrop of the moonlight you get a view into your correction. It's a metaphysical X-ray of yourself. In this way, you get a bird's-eye view as to what part of your desire to receive for yourself alone may still inhibit your fulfillment in the coming year.

When we you read from the book of Deuteronomy in the Torah, we you connect to a very specific energy that was first opened up by Rav Isaac Luria, and has only been revealed to the modern world in the past 20 or 30 years to the modern world. Prior to that, it has was always been concealed.

The purpose of the reading is to tap into the technology of anti-matter, and to embed that technology into your consciousness.

You may not understand a word of this reading—but trust me, your essence will understand everything. You will receive Light. In your true being, your 99 percent self, you will capture all of it.

You just need to absorb the words -- , and the reality of anti-matter will enter your consciousness. You don't have to understand it intellectually. You don't have to study it at Harvard.

Here' is all you need to know: Eeverything that we experience as pain, suffering, blockage, or even tragedy is time, space, and motion., Anti-matter erases the limits of time, space, and motion. The limits no longer exist. This is where we you are right now, and this is what is about to happen. This is why we you study all night. By not sleeping, we you go against the ordinary needs of the body, and we tap into the extraordinary energy of anti-matter.

So we need to pay careful attention to each and every single word in the reading. If you can, read it aloud or listen to someone who can read it in Hebrew. No matter how you engage this reading, you will connect with an energy that is absolutely chaos free.

Simchat
TORAH

he Zohar asks why this holiday has two
names: *Shemini Atzeret* (the Eighth Day of
Assembly) and *Simchat Torah* (the holiday
on which we dance with the Torah). Why is it called *"zeman
simchatenu,"* the time of our rejoicing, although we received the
Torah on *Shavuot? The Zohar* explains the name of *Simchat Torah*
with an allegory about a king who pleases his guests with a ban-
quet, only to say at the end of the meal, "And now the celebration begins!"

During *Sukkot*, we worked to impart Light to the
whole world. But why should we be concerned with the
whole world and not be satisfied merely with taking care of
our families? Once again, the Sages use an allegory to explain
this. The story is told of a dog owner who wanted to train his
dog not to eat. He began each day by giving the dog less food
than the day before until eventually he gave him no food at

all. Naturally, the dog died. Our Sages teach us that the nations of the world must be nourished, and can only be nourished, by the Israelites. This does not refer only to the People of Israel, but rather to anyone who understands and implements the wisdom of Kabbalah, which encompasses the spiritual laws of the universe. The People of Israel alone can give the world spiritual fulfillment, and therefore the world depends on them for its very existence. If the People of Israel do not look after the world, the world will have no choice but to hate them, attack them, and try to cause them to nourish it so that it does not perish from spiritual hunger. That is why the Romans, the Spaniards, and the Germans, who are all Esau's descendants, did what Nature ordered them to do. They had no choice, because the People of Israel had not performed their duty.

Joy can be revealed only when everyone is taken care of according to the principle that illuminates a lightbulb. The positive and negative poles do indeed exist, but without the resistance of the inner filament, the revelation of Light will not be achieved. Light exists in the potential state at all times, but it is not revealed without central-column resistance. Therefore, it is written in *The Zohar* that Jacob, together with the other guests, is part and parcel of *Simchat Torah*, for Jacob is central column. Thus, Jacob and restriction already exist on *Simchat Torah*. After working on this for the entire holiday, we can now enjoy the Light.

This happiness is indiscriminate, for it is the revelation of all of the Light. In this sense, the holiday is like a wedding.

Everyone who comes to the wedding—even those who have not themselves prepared the event—can participate in the celebration. Light is revealed as it was on *Shavuot*, when the Ten Utterances were given. On *Simchat Torah*, however, all the Light of the Torah is revealed—even for people who were not stringent about fulfilling all the communications on *Rosh Hashanah*, *Yom Kippur*, and *Sukkot*—because of the presence of the central column. Like a wedding, *Simchat Torah* is a time of joining between *Zeir Anpin* and *Malchut*. The bride, the groom, and their families have taken pains preparing the event, but all the guests can certainly enjoy the party. It is just like the person who turns on the light in a room; everyone who enters the room can enjoy the light for free. Therefore, everyone can receive, provided that everyone is conscious of being one with all those present. Everyone who is receiving is also willing to share, like party guests who bring the groom and bride a gift and make them happy as well.

There is no explanation in the Torah for the name *atzeret* (gathering or assembly), and there is no explicit reason for the celebration of this holiday. Only *The Zohar* explains that *atzeret* comes from the word *atzirah* (stopping). This refers to resistance, the central column, and Jacob. In addition, the meaning of the word *atzeret* is "gathering," for on this holiday all the Light assembles. Therefore, we first perform spiritual work during *Sukkot*. Later, on the eighth day, comes the holiday of the *Atzeret*, for the gathering and uncovering of all the Light. On the day of *Simchat Torah*, we receive Surrounding Light for the entire year. Only by letting go of what we now have is it possible to receive an entire year's portion of life. By holding on to what we have, we prevent the Light from entering our lives and are therefore destined to lose it all.

On *Simchat Torah*, Kabbalah teaches that we are able to cure cancer and other grave diseases. How is this possible? We know that every illness exists only as long as the body is alive. Illnesses thrive on the life processes that take place in the body; therefore, the moment a person dies, all disease in his body ceases. This principle applies to all difficulties we encounter in life. If we could skip over the processes in the physical world and rise above the illusion of the time-space continuum, we would enter a postmortem state and thus bring immediate extinction to all manifestations of chaos in our lives. *Simchat Torah* is just such an opportunity. On this holiday, we rise above the illusion of time, for *Simchat Torah* is Surrounding Light—a union of past, present, and future—and therefore constitutes an unmatched opportunity to rid our lives of all chaos.

Our main problem in the realization of this wonderful potential lies in the chronic skepticism of the human being. This skepticism tells us that anything simple cannot possibly be real. If you tell a skeptical person that tomorrow at ten o'clock the bank will be open for anyone to take as much money as they want, he will not come, for he will not believe that such a thing is possible.

On *Simchat Torah* we receive our Surrounding Light for the entire year—but then, heaven forbid, Satan comes and whispers, "If you really have received it all on *Simchat Torah*, where is it? Show it to me." In this way doubt is introduced, and the Light will disappear. We must therefore be like a man who has been told that money has been put away in a safe for him, to be received 365 days from now. This man will not be worried and will not think that he does not have the money, for he knows that the money is there for him. The same holds true for the all-inclusive surrounding Light—yesterday, today and tomorrow, beyond space and motion, without separation. Everything is there for us. We need only have certainty in its existence.

We must tear the illusions away from ourselves, cancel all of our limiting presuppositions, abolish all prejudices and doubts, and let the Light in. This is important every day, but especially on *Simchat Torah*.

Rosh Chodesh

MAR CHESHVAN

(THE SIGN OF SCORPIO AND NOAH'S FLOOD)

braham the Patriarch tells us that the month of Cheshvan is related to the sign of Scorpio. From what we know about scorpions, this suggests there is much to fear. The scorpion is the only animal that kills itself when frightened. Therefore, we must closely examine how Kabbalah can help us make our lives a bit easier, and in particular rid our lives of the fear that is so prevalent.

In order to understand the power of this month and connect to it, we will return to *the Book of Formation*, written by Abraham the Patriarch, the most ancient astrology book in the world.

Abraham and Rav Shimon Bar Yochai, in The Zohar, show us that without astrology it is very difficult to rid our lives of chaos. In *the Book of Formation*, Abraham states that the month of *Mar Cheshvan*, as well as all the stars that form the constellation referred to as Scorpio, were created from this seed. *Mar* in Hebrew means "bitter." On Shabbat, when we bless the month, we call it *Mar Cheshvan* and not *Cheshvan*. Where does the bitterness come from?

During this month, we read in the Torah about the Great Flood. Some say that the name *Mar Cheshvan* comes as a reminder of the bitterness of Noah's time. But why has Abraham chosen to remind us of the Deluge? And what about all of the other disasters that have taken place in the past? Why did Abraham seemingly decide to add a piece of "history" to the name of this month?

The Deluge flooded the world with water and destroyed it. But water has the internal energy of *Chesed*. Water conducts the Light, the force of life. That is why the human body is made mostly of water. Why, then, did the Creator choose water as the means for world destruction?

At the time, the world was full of "thievery." The Torah chose this word thousands of years ago in order to describe chaos and corruption. In order to remove the corruption and darkness, the Creator chose to flood the world with water, which conducts the power of the Light better than any other medium.

WATER

Why did Abraham see fit to name this month using the four letters נ ו שׁ ח (*Chet, Shin Vav, Nun*)? We know that each letter of the Hebrew alphabet has its own unique power. The power of *Cheshvan* remains a mystery to all those who don't study Kabbalah.

In order for those of us who do study Kabbalah to decipher this mystery, another puzzle (and a very surprising one) must first be solved: Why is the fetus surrounded by water? Scientists can tell us only that this is part of the fetal growth process. But why?

We know today that embryos are resistant and immune to all disease, particularly to cancer. Science shows us that the fetus has many more cancerous cells than any adult who suffers from the disease, and yet the fetus rejects each and every spark of cancer the moment it is formed.

What is the secret of the fetus's power? The answer lies in the revelation of an additional secret: the ancient custom of Mikveh—immersion in rejuvenating waters—known to kabbalists for millennia.

The knowledge of the Mikveh's power has been kept secret for centuries, and the concept of immersing in a Mikveh of water is a tradition that has almost disappeared today. Immersion in the Mikveh removes negative energies to a certain distance. The spiritual cleanliness obtained by immersion dramatically improves the performance of the immune system as well as the overall functioning of the body. It is even possible to reverse the aging process and to achieve recovery from illnesses that were once considered incurable. This is why the fetus grows in amniotic fluid—which, once again, is primarily water.

THE SECRET OF
THE MONTH'S NAME

At the time of the Great Flood, the entire world was afflicted with chaos to such an extent that the Creator had to flood the world with His Light. In order to do so, He used the medium that best conducts Light: the energy of *Chesed*, which is expressed by water. Today, as in the past, the month of *Cheshvan* conducts the power of Light in such a way that it can dispel all negativity from the world. Just as it did at the time of the Deluge, however, it does so with the attribute of judgment.

The month of *Cheshvan* follows the tremendous energy of *Rosh Hashanah*, *Yom Kippur*, and *Sukkot*. These occasions do not occur for the sake of tradition, but rather as tools to use during the month of *Cheshvan*.

Now the secret of the month's name may be revealed. The numerical value of חֶשְׁוָן is 364. This is a clue from Abraham as to the inner essence of *Cheshvan*. For one day a year, chaos hangs a sign on the door that says, "Out to lunch." Chaos can reign for only 364 days a year, not for 365. Thus, the month of *Cheshvan* has the power to rid and cleanse the world of chaos.

Inversion of the letters מ ר (mar) of the name וֹ ו שׁ ו ן (*Mar Cheshvan*) results in the word ר מ (ram), or lofty. What is high about this month? It is the force of life, the Light of the Creator. The month of *Cheshvan* was intended to manifest the Light that we revealed during the month of Tishrei. On the New Moon of the month of *Cheshvan*, the seed for the protective shield is sown, like the fluid in a woman's womb, in order to immerse us in the universe's protection and embrace us with the Creator's goodness. The sign of Scorpio offers us an opportunity to obtain this protective force. The objective of the communication that takes place on the *Rosh* Chodesh is to give us control over the way Light manifests in our lives, so that we may become purified in the way that the Mikveh and the amniotic fluid purify—and not, heaven forbid, by a deluge.

THE TRUE POWER OF SHARING

Why did Abraham assign the constellation of Scorpio to the month of *Cheshvan*?

In order to connect to the internal essence of the issue, we must again begin by analyzing its Hebrew name. The word עַ קְ ר בׁ (*Akrav*, meaning scorpion or Scorpio) contains the combination עַ בׁ, *Ayin-Bet* (= 72), referring to the 72 Names of God, which aid us in performing miracles.

This positive combination surrounds the letters *Kof-Resh* קׁ ר (or *kar*, meaning cold, lifeless). This technique of encircling a negative entity with positive essences is familiar from the

Shofar blowing performed during the month of Tishrei. When Abraham chose the word *Akrav*, or scorpion, he chose the word *kar*, which is wrapped by Ayin and Bet, so as to drive the coldness of death out of our lives.

A dead person becomes cold because the life processes that warm the body cease after death. Cold, however, also has the power to preserve, like a freezer. Abraham wanted to show us that when we gather together on *Rosh* Chodesh *Cheshvan*, we have ample opportunity to influence all the other 364 days of the year.

Can it be so simple? Yes! And this was Abraham's objective: to provide us with a simple and effective means of controlling our lives and our destinies. The phrase "too good to be true" is a weapon that the Opponent uses to dissuade us from using the tools. This is the loftiest, highest month of the year. In order to remove chaos, the Creator saw fit to use water, the essential medium of sharing. The Deluge did not occur in order to destroy the world, but rather to heal it of chaos and corruption. As long as we are inconsiderate toward others and do not share, however, the world has no chance.

Only sharing—that is, *Chesed*, or water—can help the world extricate itself from crisis and illness. Medical science merely replaces one illness with another. Only the consciousness of sharing with others—and not just those whom we love—can help. The concept that one must be a "good person" never helped anyone banish chaos and negativity. But the idea that he who shares receives more than does the recipient not only works, but also has no alternative. This is the only way for us to feel that we are in a protective water bubble, as in a womb. This is the only way to connect to the power that water alone can give: the divine power within, which removes chaos.

The sign of Scorpio is one of the three water signs. This month, we set up an immune system that is based on sharing. We do not want to set up this immune system through a violent and fearful event such as a deluge, but rather through a water consciousness that surrounds us, efficiently and thoroughly removing chaos from all aspects of our being.

Death Anniversary of
RACHEL
THE MATRIARCH

*O*n the 11th day of *Cheshvan*, we celebrate the birthdays of Rachel and of her youngest son, Benjamin. We say "celebrate" because, to us, a celebration is a connection to energy. We know that at the time of birth, the baby's first breath expresses the supreme spiritual level of *Keter* and is the root of all that will take place in the future. So we celebrate the birthday in order to connect to that energy of the seed. This connection is enjoyed not only by the celebrant, but also by everyone around him or her.

Righteous people depart this world when they complete their *tikkun*. Rachel was righteous, and she left this world on her birthday. Since she died while delivering her son, the 11th of *Cheshvan* is Benjamin's birthday as well as Rachel's.

RACHEL AND THE ENERGY
OF JUDGMENT

These words, written Rachel's completion of *tikkun*, were
not mentioned about any other righteous person—not even
about Abraham, although it is clear to us that Abraham completed
the *tikkun* for which he had come into the world. What, then, is
the special message that the Torah conveys to us by means of
Rachel's unique story?

When we read this biblical story literally, it is easy for us
to be filled with sadness about the tragedy of Jacob and Rachel.
Their love was great, yet they waited years until finally marrying.
They then waited for years until succeeding in having children,
and on the way to Beit Lechem, during the birth of their son,
Rachel died. But Rachel, Jacob, and Benjamin were not at all
sad, for they knew that death was nothing but an illusion, and
that physical life is nothing but a chain of opportunities with
which to progress in the *tikkun* process, like acts in a play.

Since this secret is known to all who have studied
Kabbalah, we too are no longer sad when we read the story of
Rachel's death. When an ordinary person dies, all that remains
is the inscription engraved on a tombstone. But the Patriarchs
and Matriarchs were not ordinary human beings; they were
chariots. They came into the world to become channels for the
Light of the Creator, which is revealed through the Tree of Life.
The purpose of the connection to the Tree of Life, which is a
certain connection to the Light and absolute truth, is to spare us
the ups and downs that characterize the world of Illusion.

Each and every moment in the lives of the Patriarchs and the Matriarchs had an eternal purpose. Rachel died because at that time there was judgment in the world. By means of her son and her husband, who served as connecting links between judgment and mercy, Rachel opened for us a channel of positive energy that reduces judgment and connects us to the Tree of Life.

THE RED STRING

Rav Brandwein, my teacher, experienced an event similar to the passing away of Rachel. Rav Brandwein's first wife died during the delivery of twins, a daughter and a son, and years later this same daughter died in labor as well. There is no doubt that we have here a clear case of judgment. In light of such events, *The Zohar* asks, "What then is the purpose of the story of Rachel's death?" And it answers: From this story, we can convert the revelation of judgment in our lives into right-column energy—that is, into the energy of *Chesed*, which is the power of life and blessing.

Rachel is not buried with Jacob and the other Patriarchs, but rather along the road between Jerusalem and Beit Lechem. *The Zohar* explains that Rachel is buried by herself because, when one is alone, one can feel other people. When you are in the company of other people all the time, how can you connect with any one individual? But those who are buried on the side of the road, in an exposed location, enable others to make contact and seek assistance.

Rachel and Jacob knew that Rachel was meant to serve as a channel of caring, (*deagah*) for all generations, right up until the Resurrection of the Dead. It is written that Rachel is " . . . weeping for her children . . . " (Jeremiah 31:14)—for she is our channel for care and concern. Rachel is related to the lower triangle of the Shield of David, and therefore we have direct access to her. We are all Rachel's children, and when she weeps, she weeps for us all.

On the other hand, Rachel's sister, Leah, was buried in the Cave of Machpelah in Hebron. She is related to the upper triangle of the Shield of David, and therefore she has no direct linkage to the realm of *Malchut* or to the troubles we face in the physical world. Since Jacob was elevated to the level of Israel, he cut himself off from *Malchut* and was therefore buried in Hebron, beside Leah, and not beside Rachel, his beloved wife.

It is now easy to understand why we wind the Red String—which brings protection from negative energy—at Rachel's tomb and nowhere else. Only Rachel, with love and with true and infinite caring, has the power to transmit to us all full protection against the Evil Eye and the influence of negative energies.

Joseph and Benjamin

Benjamin was born during the month of *Mar Cheshvan* because it is a month of Judgment, or *Din*. All those born in this month will testify that it does not come with an easy *tikkun*. But

Mar (bitter) does not mean evil. Medications usually taste bitter, but they are nonetheless essential to the process of recovering from illness. We have said that *Rosh* Chodesh *Mar Cheshvan* is the most powerful day of the year, but the death anniversary of Rachel is no less powerful. Furthermore, today we have the ability to reduce the judgment of *Mar Cheshvan* and turn it into Ram (high) *Cheshvan*, the most positive time of the year.

How is this possible? It is because on the death anniversary of righteous people we connect to all the positive energy they revealed during their entire lifetimes. Thus, on the 33rd day of the Omer (*Lag B'aomer*), the death anniversary of Rav Shimon, he reduces the judgment that is in the period of the Omer; The Ari, Rav Isaac Luria, assists us on his death anniversary on the fifth day of the month of *Av*, during the three negative weeks of the year; and Rachel performed the same service, many years before them both.

Rachel had two sons, Joseph and Benjamin, and they both attained the eternal title of righteous. This is very different from Noah, for example, who was a righteous man in his generation only, as well as from the rest of Jacob's sons, who did not earn the title of righteous at all.

For those who are not experts in Kabbalah, it may seem that children are a matter of luck. Sometimes a good child is born, and sometimes a not-so-good child is born. Occasionally a good child is born to parents who aren't good, or a not-good child is born to good parents. Terach was not a righteous man, but he nonetheless brought Abraham into the world—a chariot for Sfirat *Chesed*. King David was a chariot to Sfirat *Malchut*, and nevertheless he brought into the world Absalom, a rebellious son who attempted to murder his own father.

The Zohar reveals to us that there is a way to control this luck—to rise above the influence of the stars and determine the quality of our children. And this is precisely what we achieve by means of connection with Rachel.

Rachel, by virtue of the spiritual work she performed during her lifetime, had the privilege to rise above her natural position and connect to *Binah*. Seeing that this was so, it was certain that she would be the mother of righteous children such as Joseph and Benjamin. Using *The Zohar* and the wisdom of Kabbalah, we now have the privilege to connect to the energy Rachel brought to the world and to use it in order to improve our lives.

"Luck" and Destiny

The Zohar described the era in which we live as very positive and yet very negative at the same time. At this time, great Light will flood the universe. Those who have not prepared and developed an appropriate spiritual vessel will be struck by the excess of Light, known by the name of Judgment. At exactly the same time, all those who will expand and develop their spiritual vessel to a certain extent, using the consciousness embodied in *The Zohar*, will gain complete and merciful Redemption. For them, the days of the Messiah will the most wonderful of times.

The connection to Rachel enables a balanced connection between *Malchut* and *Binah*, and therefore enables us to control "luck." When Rachel conceived for the second time, Jacob and Rachel knew that they would have a son, that Rachel would die in the course of his delivery, and that the 12 sons would complete the system for control over the 12 signs of the zodiac. Each of the first 11 sons, however, ruled only one sign of the zodiac. Benjamin, the last son, controlled not only the 12th sign but the entire zodiac itself. This is because all of Jacob's sons except Benjamin were born outside of Israel. Laban tried to detain Jacob so that Benjamin would be born outside of Israel as well, but Jacob knew that the only way the Israelites would be able to control their destiny would be if Benjamin were to be born in Yisrael. Therefore, he freed himself from Laban's control and fled to Israel.

All of the Patriarchs' lives, in every detail and every day and every moment, were dedicated to imparting unto us tools for the control over destiny.

Death Anniversary of
RABBI
AVRAHAM AZULAI

*E*ach year, when we come to the anniversary of Rav Avraham Azulai's decision to leave this world, I think about how different I was before I came to Kabbalah. For instance, I had never heard the name Avraham Azulai. Even now, outside the Kabbalah Centres around the world, most people don't even know he existed.

Only when I met my teacher, Rav Brandwein, and learned the purpose of the Centre, did I understand what Rav Brandwein and Rav Ashlag before him had been working to achieve. I learned also how the work of the Centre was so closely connected to Rav Azulai.

Rabbi Brandwein taught me that Avraham Azulai, hundreds of years ago, had foreseen the time when Kabbalah not only *would* no longer be concealed, but *must* no longer be concealed.

All the time that the Israelites were in exile in history, we were commanded to hide the wisdom. Now, when we have to prepare ourselves for the coming of meshiach, the wisdom of Kabbalah needs to be revealed. Avraham Azulai was quite explicit about this. The prohibition on the study of Kabbalah was in force only until the year 5250, after which everyone was permitted to study the Zohar and the other teachings.

It is very important that people as a whole, old and young, should study the Kabbalah. By *study* we don't mean just an intellectual understanding of the teachings. Study means connection with the Light and revelation of the Light. The anniversary of Avraham Azulai's leaving this world is our opportunity to accomplish this and to help to bring to an end negativity in any form.

With respect to the Zohar, even if we don't know a single word of Hebrew, we can study simply by scanning the words or by hearing them read aloud. Merely by seeing or listening to the words, we arouse the true dimension of the Light of God. Today, thanks to the efforts of Michael Berg, we have the first complete English translations of the Zohar and Rav Ashlag's commentary on the Zohar.

A person should study the Zohar day and night. Why at every moment? Because in every moment of study, Light that reveals an entire universe is revealed. That happens simply because one person indulges in this study.

In regard to this, Rav Azulai made a very powerful statement: Any changes we make in our lives, no matter how positive they may be, pale in comparison to reading the Zohar in terms of bringing an end to chaos in the world. We might say that reading the Zohar arouses within us the idea of sharing. We might say that reading the Zohar allows us to be better human beings. We might say it helps us to share. Nothing is more powerful or important than the Light that is revealed simply by the act of reading itself.

This is what Avraham Azulai taught us. We have so much to be thankful for in the deeds of the righteous, and we owe thanks to Rav Azulai for giving the world access to the tools of Kabbalah. By connecting with his presence, reading his writings, and studying Kabbalah in the true meaning of the word *study*, we will achieve the ultimate and permanent removal of suffering, chaos, and death.

Rosh Chodesh
KISLEV ·
(JUPITER AND SAGITTARIUS)

*E*ach month, the New Moon contains the potential for the entire month to come. On this day we have the ability to direct, nurture, and shape all coming events. The letters of the month of *Kislev* are ܘ (*Samech*) and ܐ (*Gimel*). The thought consciousness represented by the letter *Samech* created the sign of Sagittarius, and the one represented by the letter *Gimel* created Jupiter, the largest planet in the solar system. The numerical value of *Samech* and *Gimel* is 63, which is also the numerical value of a special spelling-out of the *Yud Hei Vav Hei*, the Name that connects us with the *Sfirah* of *Binah*.

Our task in this month lies in disseminating the knowledge given to us by Abraham the Patriarch in *the Book of Formation* 4,000 years ago. Through the letters of this month, we can gain control over the planet Jupiter and its astrological sign so that we may succeed in manifesting their positive aspects.

The month of *Kislev* is a month of miracles. The Miracle of *Chanukah* is the result of cosmic forces that are transmitted each year via Sagittarius and Jupiter. By means of the knowledge we receive from Abraham, it is possible for us to attract these forces and to materialize them in the world. Using this power, it is possible for us to turn chaotic reality into blessing and harmony. This is the essence of miracle making.

Through meditation with the letters of the month, it is possible to reveal the Light of the Creator in our own lives as individuals, as well as to remove chaos and any manifestation of Satan consciousness from the world as a whole.

Miracles and Immortality

Approximately 400 years ago, Rav Avraham Azulai canceled the edict that had restricted the study of Kabbalah. Rav Azulai's writings have also given us the understanding that it is possible in our time to achieve Bila Hamavet Lanetzach—the "death of death"—forever. In fact, as we begin to contemplate this possibility, information has begun to appear in scientific publications as well as in the general media regarding medical discoveries that confirm Rav Azulai's forecast.

These discoveries are related primarily to cancer research. It seems that cancerous tissue makes use of the immense power of Bila Hamavet Lanetzach in order to spread and multiply in an unrestrained fashion. Within cancerous cells, an "immortality" gene has been found that is responsible for the cells' renewal capability.

These discoveries have far-reaching implications. Through them we recognize the human body's physiologic ability to reconstruct, from the genetic code found in cell nuclei, any organ and any tissue. This includes even limbs that have been amputated as a result of an accident as well as those that have been surgically removed. The body also has the hidden ability to renew itself at any age in a way that overcomes the phenomenon of aging and creates eternal life with perfect health.

In order to achieve all this, we must purify ourselves during the entire year—especially in the month of *Kislev*, within which exists the ability to create miracles. Throughout the entire month, it is crucial that we maintain a consciousness of patience, sensitivity, and concern for others. Those who comply with these conditions will remain pure, and only in this way may they come close to the Creator, reveal Light in the world, and perform miracles. It is important to remember that we are all sons and daughters of the universal family, and that each and every one of us has the capability to contribute in a unique manner to the benefit of all members of that family.

Our True Tasks

We must cast away all dissension and hatred and concentrate instead on the truly important tasks: bringing peace, eternal life, and resurrection of the dead to the world. Only now can these things be attained by virtue of the cosmic window of opportunity that has opened before us in this era.

Impatience and intolerance are our greatest enemies. Rather than feverishly attempting to impose our opinions on the world, it is better for us to join hands with people who think differently from us, and together bring blessing and benefit to all mankind. Removing fragmentation from human experience requires abolishing hatred toward all those whose opinions differ from our own. This hatred caused the Holocaust and brought about the destruction of The Temple and the 2,000-year exile.

Hatred cannot come from the Light. As Kabbalah teaches, within the Light there is a unity of variance: "And there was evening and there was morning, day one" (*Beresheet* 1:5). Only on the second day were *Chesed* and *Gvurah* created. Separation exists only outside the Light, not within it. *Chesed* does not contradict *Gvurah*, and *Gvurah* does not contradict *Chesed*; rather, these two aspects express two faces of the Light, and the harmonious integration of the two brings life to the world.

During the Binding of Isaac, we learned that even when Abraham thought that the Creator wanted him to sacrifice Isaac, the angel of God came and said that, no, this was not the meaning. It was only a code to teach us that we must apply restriction of the desire to receive for the self alone. This is what the Binding of Isaac teaches us.

By virtue of truly righteous people such as the Kabbalist Rav Avraham Azulai, we will succeed in bringing unity and peace to the entire world. This revelation of Light will enable scientific and medical development such that immortality will come to be common property, not an exotic biblical concept. But the responsibility for this achievement rests on us all. Only Kabbalah can purify man from the malignant illness called hatred for no reason—a sickness that has plagued the world for thousands of years. Using Kabbalah, we can destroy negative consciousness, eradicate from within ourselves the seed of death, and even achieve the resurrection of the dead.

MORE FROM RAV P. S. BERG

Wheels of a Soul
By Rav Berg

In *Wheels of a Soul*, Kabbalist Rav Berg reveals the keys to answering these and many more questions that lie at the heart of our existence as human beings. Specifically, Rav Berg explains why we must acknowledge and explore the lives we have already lived in order to understand the life we are living today . . .

Make no mistake: *you have been here before*. Reincarnation is a fact—and just as science is now beginning to recognize that time and space may be nothing but illusions, Rav Berg shows why death itself is the greatest illusion of all.

In this book you learn much more than the answers to these questions. You will understand your true purpose in the world and discover tools to identify your life's soul mate. Read *Wheels of a Soul* and let one of the greatest kabbalistic masters of our time change your life forever.

The Power of You
By Rav Berg

For the past 5,000 years, neither science nor psychology has been able to solve the fundamental problem of chaos in people's lives.

Now, one man is providing the answer. He is Kabbalist Rav Berg.

Beneath the pain and chaos that disrupts our lives, Kabbalist Rav Berg brings to light a hidden realm of order, purpose, and unity. Revealed is a universe in which mind becomes master over matter—a world in which God, human thought, and the entire cosmos are mysteriously interconnected.

Join this generation's premier kabbalist on a mind-bending journey along the cutting edge of reality. Peer into the vast reservoir of spiritual wisdom that is Kabbalah, where the secrets of creation, life, and death have remained hidden for thousands of years.

The Essential Zohar
By Rav Berg

The Zohar has traditionally been known as the world's most esoteric and profound spiritual document, but Kabbalist Rav Berg, this generation's greatest living Kabbalist, has dedicated his life to making this wisdom universally available. The vast wisdom and Light of *The Zohar* came into being as a gift to all humanity, and *The Essential Zohar* at last explains this gift to the world.

THE ZOHAR

"Bringing *The Zohar* from near oblivion to wide accessibility has taken many decades. It is an achievement of which we are truly proud and grateful."

—Michael Berg

Composed more than 2,000 years ago, *The Zohar* is a set of 23 books, a commentary on biblical and spiritual matters in the form of conversations among spiritual masters. But to describe *The Zohar* only in physical terms is greatly misleading. In truth, *The Zohar* is nothing less than a powerful tool for achieving the most important purposes of our lives. It was given to all humankind by the Creator to bring us protection, to connect us with the Creator's Light, and ultimately to fulfill our birthright of true spiritual transformation.

More than eighty years ago, when The Kabbalah Centre was founded, *The Zohar* had virtually disappeared from the world. Few people in the general population had ever heard of it. Whoever sought to read it—in any country, in any language, at any price—faced a long and futile search.

Today all this has changed. Through the work of The Kabbalah Centre and the editorial efforts of Michael Berg, *The Zohar* is now being brought to the world, not only in the original Aramaic language but also in English.

The new English Zohar provides everything for connecting to this sacred text on all levels: the original Aramaic text for scanning; an English translation; and clear, concise commentary for study and learning.

MORE BOOKS THAT CAN BRING THE WISDOM OF KABBALAH INTO YOUR LIFE

God Wears Lipstick
By Karen Berg

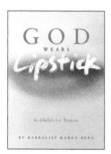

God Wears Lipstick is written exclusively for women (or for men who better want to understand women) by one of the driving forces behind the Kabbalah movement.

For thousands of years, women were banned from studying Kabbalah, the ancient source of wisdom that explains who we are and what our purpose is in this universe.

Karen Berg changed that. She opened the doors of The Kabbalah Centre to anyone who wanted to understand the wisdom of Kabbalah and brought Light to these people.

In *God Wears Lipstick*, Karen Berg shares that wisdom with us, especially as it affects you and your relationships. She reveals a woman's special place in the universe and why women have a spiritual advantage over men. She explains how to find your soulmate and your purpose in life. She empowers you to become a better human being as you connect to the Light, and she then gives you the tools for living and loving.

The Power of Kabbalah
By Yehuda Berg

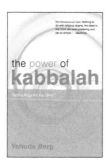

Imagine your life filled with unending joy, purpose, and contentment. Imagine your days infused with pure insight and energy. This is *The Power of Kabbalah*. It is the path from the momentary pleasure that most of us settle for, to the lasting fulfillment that is yours to claim. Your deepest desires are waiting to be realized. But they are not limited to the temporary rush from closing a business deal, the short-term high from drugs, or a passionate sexual relationship that lasts only a few short months.

Wouldn't you like to experience a lasting sense of wholeness and peace that is unshakable, no matter what may be happening around you? Complete fulfillment is the promise of Kabbalah. Within these pages, you will learn how to look at and navigate through life in a whole new way. You will understand your purpose and how to receive the abundant gifts waiting for you. By making a critical transformation from a reactive to a proactive being, you will increase your creative energy, get control of your life, and enjoy new spiritual levels of existence. Kabbalah's ancient teaching is rooted in the perfect union of the physical and spiritual laws already at work in your life. Get ready to experience this exciting realm of awareness, meaning, and joy.

The wonder and wisdom of Kabbalah has influenced the world's leading spiritual, philosophical, religious, and scientific minds. Until today, however, it was hidden away in ancient texts, available only to scholars who knew where to look. Now after many centuries, *The Power of Kabbalah* resides right here in this one remarkable book. Here, at long last is the complete and simple path—actions you can take right now to create the life you desire and deserve.

Becoming Like God
By Michael Berg

At the age of 16, kabbalistic scholar Michael Berg began the herculean task of translating *The Zohar*, Kabbalah's chief text, from its original Aramaic into its first complete English translation. *The Zohar*, which consists of 23 volumes, is considered a compendium of virtually all information pertaining to the universe, and its wisdom is only beginning to be verified today.

During the ten years he worked on *The Zohar*, Michael Berg discovered the long-lost secret for which humanity has searched for more than 5,000 years: how to achieve our ultimate destiny. *Becoming Like God* reveals the transformative method by which people can actually break free of what is called "ego nature" to achieve total joy and lasting life.

Berg puts forth the revolutionary idea that for the first time in history, an opportunity is being made available to humankind: an opportunity to Become Like God.

The Secret
By Michael Berg

Like a jewel that has been painstakingly cut and polished, *The Secret* reveals life's essence in its most concise and powerful form. Michael Berg begins by showing you how our everyday understanding of our purpose in the world is literally backwards. Whenever there is pain in our lives—indeed, whenever there is anything less than complete joy and fulfillment—this basic misunderstanding is the reason.

The Red String: The Power of Protection
By Yehuda Berg

Read the book that everyone is wearing!

Discover the ancient technology that empowers and fuels the hugely popular Red String, the most widely recognized tool of kabbalistic wisdom. Yehuda Berg, author of the international best-seller *The 72 Names of God: Technology for the Soul*, continues to reveal the secrets of the world's oldest and most powerful wisdom with his new book, *The Red String: The Power of Protection*. Discover the antidote to the negative effects of the dreaded "Evil Eye" in this second book of the Technology for the Soul series.

Find out the real power behind the Red String and why millions of people won't leave home without it.

It's all here. Everything you wanted to know about the Red String but were afraid to ask!

THE KABBALAH CENTRE

The International Leader in the Education of Kabbalah

Since its founding, The Kabbalah Centre has had a single mission: to improve and transform people's lives by bringing the power and wisdom of Kabbalah to all who wish to partake of it.

Through the lifelong efforts of Kabbalists Rav and Karen Berg, and the great spiritual lineage of which they are a part, an astonishing 3.5 million people around the world have already been touched by the powerful teachings of Kabbalah. And each year, the numbers are growing!

• • • •

If you were inspired by this book in any way and would like to know how you can continue to enrich your life through the wisdom of Kabbalah, here is what you can do next:

Call 1-800-KABBALAH where trained instructors are available 18 hours a day. These dedicated people are willing to answer any and all questions about Kabbalah and help guide you along in your effort to learn more.

For our children

Michael, Mordechay, and Esther

and for our teachers

Harav, Karen, Yehuda and Michael.